CHURCHES AND
CATHEDRALS

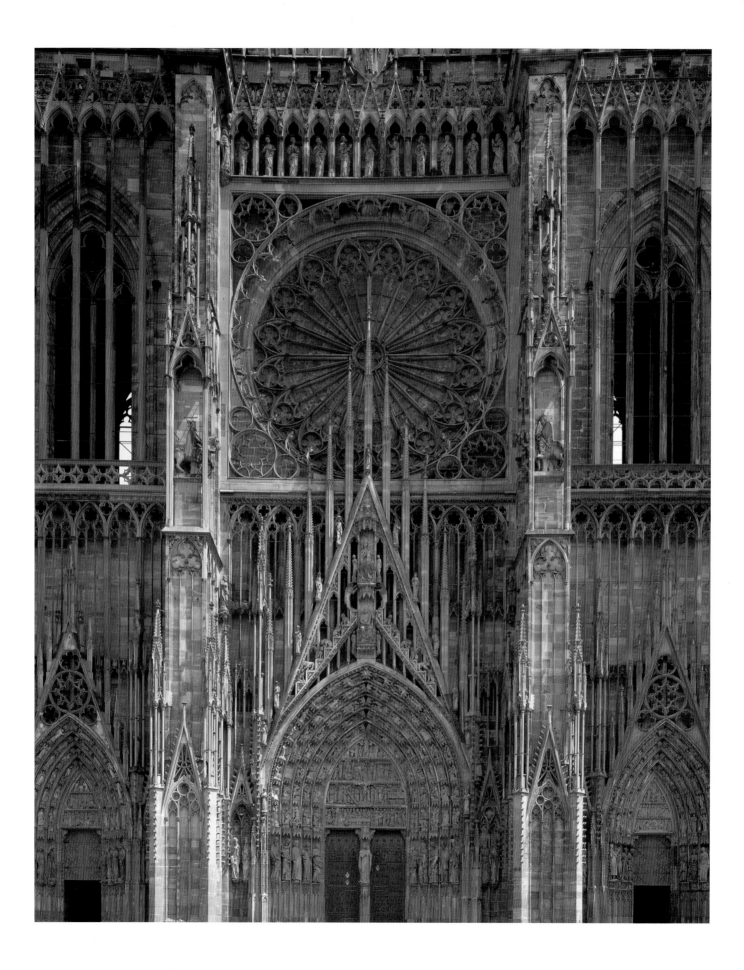

Churches and CATHEDRALS

1700 Years of the Most Beautiful Architecture

Edited by Rolf Toman

Text by Barbara Borngässer

Photographs by Achim Bednorz

Bath New York Singapore Hong Kong Cologne Delhi Melbourne

CONTENTS

Editor's Foreword
6

The Early Christian and Byzantine Eras
8

Sacred Architecture of the Carolingian, Ottonian,
and Romanesque Periods
18

The Gothic Period
80

The Renaissance
168

Baroque, Rococo, and Neoclassicism
190

Historicism and Modernism
236

EDITOR'S FOREWORD

Among the construction that took place during the medieval period in Europe, a span of approximately a thousand years and the subject of the largest portion of this volume, the building of Christian churches occupied the most prominent position. Among the countless church structures of the Middle Ages, the most outstanding in terms of size and splendor (with very few exceptions) are the great cathedrals. Also called domes in Germany and Italy (*Dom* or *duomo*, respectively), and minsters (*Münster*) in southern Germany and Austria, in the strictest sense of the term, these represent bishops' churches. "Cathedra" refers to the throne-like chair of the bishop at the Pontifical High Mass; it is simultaneously a symbol of the bishop's distinguished position in the official Church hierarchy. The terms "dome" or "minster," however, were sometimes applied to certain parish churches—and even a few abbey churches—in order to endow them with an honorable title in keeping with their extraordinary size or artistic status.

In the three centuries from 1050 to 1350, unimaginable quantities of stone were obtained and shaped for the purpose of constructing "eighty cathedrals, 500 large churches, and tens of thousands of parish churches" in France alone. Medievalist Jean Gimpel writes of several million tons of stone that were transported there. He also points out the considerable areas of land that the numerous houses of worship occupied in the cities of the Middle Ages: "With a surface area of almost 83,000 square feet (7,700 m²), the Cathedral of Amiens was so large that it was possible for the entire population of the city—approximately ten thousand people—to take part in a single ceremony."

"Did so many people ever really come to church?" a contemporary skeptic might ask. We can find an answer in the writings of Suger, the abbot and initiator of the new construction of the Royal Abbey Church of St-Denis: "On feast days, the basilica was often so full that the crowds swelled back out of the door. . . . As astonishing as it might sound, one could sometimes observe such a throng of people pressing back against those who were just entering to honor and kiss the holy relics—the Savior's nails and His crown of thorns—that none of the thousands of people could take even the smallest step, so tightly were they pressed together." Feast days of this kind occurred frequently enough in medieval times. Nowadays, such a crush might only be expected at an important state funeral or at Easter Mass in St Peter's. The tremendous efforts people went to in those days to build this multitude of gigantic houses of worship is only fathomable against the background of the religious fervor that existed in the Middle Ages. The people not only made monetary donations for the construction of the churches, they also made practical contributions by carting materials or engaging in other forms of voluntary labor. Even members of the nobility were said to have been active in this way. Thus, in the Middle Ages, piety and religious ardor were driving forces that should not be underestimated.

Nevertheless, there were also other reasons, primarily economic, for the construction boom. Most of the large-scale projects, including some of the abbey churches of the mendicant Franciscan and Dominican orders, were carried out in up-and-coming cities where a society with an increasingly differentiated division of labor had acquired some wealth. The Church was more or less opposed to this new, urban profit-seeking; at the same time, it knew how to take advantage of people's increasing prosperity. The approach was not necessarily strategic or intentionally deceitful; rather, it was completely in line with the logic of bartering between earthly possessions and heavenly salvation—an element of universal religious belief without which the method could not have succeeded. People who had acquired material wealth were burdened with guilt, and the Church unburdened them by offering atonement for their sins in return for the donation of part of their assets or legacy to religious causes, including the construction of churches. However, this represented only one side of the coin.

The other aspect of the issue was a kind of medieval civic pride that mobilized people's desire to contribute to their city. The people of the middle class, who had achieved a degree of freedom previously unknown, were proud of their cities' splendor, of their houses, and not least of the size and magnificence of their churches. The tall towers of the cathedrals and parish churches proclaimed the stature of these sacred buildings far and wide. Likewise, the interiors of the churches were resplendent with donated furnishings. The donors enjoyed erecting monuments to their own generosity, as in the brilliant glasswork of an expensive church window, for example, a favorite vehicle for self-glorification. This often took the form of a glass medallion identifying the professional status of the donor. A loaf of bread represented the baking trade, a pair of scissors that of a tailor. These symbols can be seen as an early form of image-building.

In this book, a large part of the extensive chapter on the Gothic period is devoted to the urban cathedrals of the twelfth to fourteenth centuries. Embodying the apex of Christian architecture, they also provide the title for the book as a whole, serving as a sort of shorthand for all sacred building. In general, a simple equation is often drawn between the Gothic period and the age of cathedrals. This is accurate only insofar as the construction of most—and the most famous—cathedrals took place during this era. Nevertheless, we should keep in mind that even during the Gothic period, the number of newly constructed parish and abbey churches far surpassed that of cathedrals. Furthermore, there are also cathedrals that date from the Romanesque, the Renaissance and the baroque periods.

It was the publisher's desire to present the most important cathedrals not only as a church form *sui generis* and limited to the Middle Ages, but in the context of a brief history of Christian sacred architecture from late antiquity to the present. Perforce, this overview also includes abbey, parish, and pilgrimage churches. The most important of these (and those selected for inclusion in this volume) were also built to the very highest artistic standards; hence the addendum to the book's title, "and other important church buildings of the past 1700 years."

Those years span the time between the Edict of Milan in AD 313—Emperor Constantine's guarantee of freedom for all religious groups in the Roman Empire—and the present. In the fourth century, Christianity, which had suffered bloody persecution under Diocletian (285–313), rose from this state of toleration to its proclamation as the official state religion under Theodosius the Great (379–395). Definitive and influential church buildings were constructed during this period, such as the Church of the Holy Sepulcher in Jerusalem (begun in 326) and Old St Peter's in Rome (dedicated in 326). After this, however, although there continued to be strong support for the building of churches (as was true in Palestine, Trier, and other locations), Rome relinquished its position as capital to the new metropolis of Constantinople. It was from the latter city that important impulses arose in the centuries that followed.

When one compares the magnificent structures of the early Middle Ages—only a few of which have been preserved—with those of the high and late Middle Ages, the early blossoming of sacred architecture is astonishing. The awe and wonder we experience standing before the mosaic work of S. Vitale in Ravenna is no less than that inspired by the stained glass windows of Chartres. Even someone who feels historically ill-equipped to compare the religious and cultural conditions in Byzantine Ravenna and twelfth-century Paris and its environs will be quite able to perceive the great changes in spirit that distinguish these dramatically different churches. The same can be said of the contrast between Romanesque and baroque abbey churches. Similarly, the structures created by scholarly Renaissance architects who based their designs on those of antiquity were motivated and designed quite differently than the Cistercian churches inspired by the genius of St Bernhard. What variety in the execution of a single building task! Behind every change in form we can also find a change in intellectual and spiritual outlook. This is another theme of this book: although the cultural-historical background of the works is not probed intensively, the chapter introductions still explain it sufficiently to allow readers to understand the basic relationship between the ideas of a given period—its intellectual and spiritual trends—and its sacred architecture.

Arriving at this selection of nearly 240 church structures was not easy; it could easily have been two or three times that number. When the publisher specified a number of pages for the book, we—the editor and author—decided that instead of covering a greater number of buildings, we would limit the number of churches to allow enough space for their visual presentation. Our selection is naturally somewhat subjective, shaped by particular viewpoints and aesthetic preferences. And yet it is far from arbitrary, since for every era—at least until the early modern period—it follows the canon of popular architectural history and covers the most important church structures. Of course we had to include St Peter's in Rome, Speyer Cathedral, the Cathedral of Notre-Dame in Reims, the Duomo in Florence, a church building by Palladio in Venice, the Karlskirche in Vienna, the Sagrada Familia . . . but for the few modern churches built after 1950 our selection could certainly have been different.

Descriptions of the churches are limited to their fundamental elements—unique, style-defining or era-specific—as well as essential information about the history of their construction, the architects, and the initiating parties. This allowed sufficient space for the outstanding photographs by Achim Bednorz, a well-known specialist in the field of sacred architecture.

THE EARLY CHRISTIAN AND BYZANTINE ERAS

The Battle of the Milvian Bridge in the year 313, from which the Roman emperor Constantine emerged victorious "under the sign of the Cross," confirmed Christianity's triumph. In the same year, the Edict of Milan proclaimed an end to the persecution of Christians, and the cornerstone of St John Lateran was laid in Rome. A Roman parish church, this was also the first official bishop's seat—the first cathedral in the history of Christianity. Approximately ten years later, work was begun on St Peter's, erected over the gravesite of St Peter, martyr and Prince of the Apostles. Other incunabula of Christian architecture appeared in the fourth and fifth centuries in the churches of St Paul Outside the Walls, S. Maria Maggiore, and S. Sabina all'Aventino.

A standard form of Christian sacred architecture was taking shape during Constantine's time, and remains essentially binding to the present day: the floor plan consists of a nave with three or five side aisles, a transept, and a semicircular eastern apse. In front of the facade is a narthex, with or without an atrium.

The prototypes for these Early Christian houses of worship were, in fact, of pagan origin. The basilica form, a longitudinal room with multiple aisles and a projecting upper story, had been employed in antiquity for courthouses, reception halls, and throne rooms. Meanwhile, the rotunda—also known as *tholos*, a popular temple form—was adopted by Christians primarily for mausoleums and memorial buildings. Christian architecture thus adapted traditional models and adjusted them to fit new liturgical requirements and the influx of the faithful. Many Early Christian church buildings have been passed down to us only in greatly altered forms: the ambitions of the popes and bishops would not tolerate stagnation. Consider the ever-evolving architectural history of St Peter's, for example, or Borromini's renovations in St John Lateran (which, ingenious though they were, nevertheless obscured the original fabric of the building).

As Rome lost its preeminence at the end of the fourth century, new religious centers arose. The division of the world empire in 395 was an indication of this development. From that time on, the Eastern Roman Empire with its capital at Constantinople (Byzantium) competed with the Western Roman Empire centered in Ravenna for the legacy of the shattered *Imperium Romanum*.

In Ravenna, magnificent examples of Early Christian architecture and mosaic ornamentation have been preserved. The impact of these basilicas and their imagery extended far into the Middle Ages. Eastern Roman influences are clearly visible in the octagonal brick structure of S. Vitale, whose domed structure then served as a model for Charlemagne's Palatine Chapel in Aachen.

Under the Eastern Roman emperors, Constantinople became the "New Rome," adorning itself with fantastic churches. Hagia Sophia, with its brilliant mosaics and majestic dome that seems to float above the building, is probably the most impressive sacred structure of the first millennium. It influenced Byzantine and Western church architecture alike. After the conquest of Constantinople by the Ottoman Turks in 1493, it served as a model for the splendid mosques created by the master builder

Rome, S. Constanza, Mausoleum of Constantina, mid-fourth century, gallery with vault mosaic.

Left: **Ravenna,** S. Vitale, 526–547, detail of capital.

Opposite: **Trier,** Palatine Chapel, ca. 310, view toward the northwest. The throne room (basilica) of Emperor Constantine the Great was the prestigious center of the royal residence at Trier. At 220 ft long, 90 ft wide, and 100 ft high (67 x 27 x 30 m), this brick building was one of the most enormous of the late antique period.

Rome, S. Costanza

Constantina, daughter of Emperor Constantine, commissioned the building of a church outside the gates of Rome with an adjacent mausoleum to contain her mortal remains and those of her sister, Helena. The building, whose interior is completely lined with marble inlays and mosaics, is one of the most beautiful examples of late antique memorial architecture. Elegant granite double columns form an inner circle bordered by an ambulatory with chapels and niches. The main axes are accentuated with additional openings. The Corinthian capitals carry architraves, which act as imposts under the arches. The original building was also encircled by a colonnaded porch.

Opposite, top left: **Rome,** S. Costanza, Mausoleum of Constantina, mid-fourth century, view into the rotunda.

Rome, Old St Peter's

In about 320, on a site at the foot of the Vatican Hill, Emperor Constantine built St Peter's, the noblest church in Christendom, above the grave of St Peter, martyr and Prince of the Apostles. Measuring 295 feet long and 217 feet wide (90 x 66 m), it was also the largest of the Early Christian churches erected in Rome. Its five-aisled nave was articulated with colonnades, and its projecting transept could accommodate a huge number of the faithful. Its liturgical center was (and still is) the grave of St Peter with the shrine (or *memoria*) at the cord of the apse. A great colonnaded atrium was set in front of the main building.

From 1506 onwards, Old St Peter's was disassembled piecemeal and replaced by the new St Peter's.

Above: **Rome,** Old St Peter's, begun 320, view through the nave toward the west. Painting from the 17th century, Rome, St Peter's.

Basilicas and Rotundas

The longitudinal basilica and the rotunda were the favored forms of Early Christian sacred building. Both forms had been well established in antiquity and were adapted for Christian purposes: the basilica as a gathering space for the faithful, and the rotunda as a memorial or burial monument.

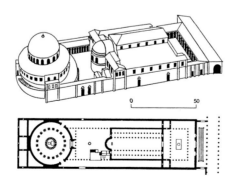

Jerusalem, Church of the Holy Sepulcher, begun 326, floor plan and reconstruction of the building under Constantine. Right to left: atrium, 5-aisled basilica, courtyard with colonnade, rotunda. The domed rotunda was copied in many central-plan buildings.

Rome, S. Sabina all'Aventino

Thanks to extensive restoration, among all the buildings in Rome, S. Sabina provides the most accurate picture of Early Christian sacred architecture. Its three-aisled, columned basilica, which still lacked any transept, guides the visitor directly to the choir with its altar and apse mosaic (not preserved). Twenty Corinthian columns—spolia from an earlier imperial Roman building—support the clerestory wall, which contains a long row of round-arched windows. The nave is enclosed by a flat wooden roof typical of the period; the side aisles provide a view into the open roof truss.

In addition to its impressive interior, S. Sabina also boasts a unique example of early Christian wood carving: the panels of the main doorway, dating from about 430, depict scenes from the Old and New Testaments.

Opposite, top right and bottom: **Rome,** S. Sabina all'Aventino, between 422 and 432, exterior and view into the interior.

Milan, S. Lorenzo Maggiore

Milan owes its extraordinary wealth of Early Christian architecture to St Ambrose. As bishop of this Lombard city from 374 to 397, he encircled its Roman center with Christian basilicas and martyria.

S. Lorenzo Maggiore lays claim to an exceptional status among these churches because the building, which is decorated with marble and rich mosaics, is thought to have been the chapel of the imperial palace. Despite numerous modifications in the twelfth and sixteenth centuries, the vaulted rotunda still reveals its late antique origins. The church is a double-shelled construction: the curved walls of the exterior structure are matched in the interior by a quatrefoil of columns, between which two-storied piers curve gently.

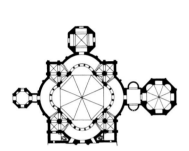

Milan, S. Lorenzo

Thessaloniki, Hagios Demetrios

Countless legends surround the Church of Hagios Demetrios in Saloniki, the ancient name for Thessaloniki or Salonica. The five-aisled basilica with its narthex, transept, and triforium was founded in the fifth century, clearly intended to accommodate huge numbers of the faithful. In contrast to other Early

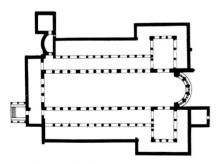

Thessaloniki, Hagios Demetrios

Christian churches, it features colonnades rhythmically interspersed with single brick piers. The church is dedicated to St Demetrius, the most famous Greek martyr and patron saint of the city. According to legend, he met his death in the heater of a public bath: the foundation walls of that facility served as the substructure of the Christian church.

The building's main attraction is a silver-plated hexagonal ciborium on the north side of the nave. Later, a fountain was "discovered" there from which—thanks to an ingenious system of pipes—aromatic oil flowed prior to the saint's feast day. Hagios Demetrios burned to the ground in 1917 and was completely reconstructed.

Top and above: **Milan,** Basilica of S. Lorenzo, third quarter of the fourth century, view into the interior and of the exterior.

Opposite: **Thessaloniki,** Hagios Demetrios, last quarter of the fifth century; reconstruction after a fire in 1917; interior view toward the west.

The magnificent impact of the interior space o[f] S. Vitale in Ravenna lends it a special status among Early Christian centrally planned churches. This brick building can be traced back to a donation by the banker Julianus Argentarius. It was begun around 526, at almost the same time as its immediate proto-type, the Church of Hagios Sergios and Bakchos in Constantinople. That church is also a double-shelled octagon with galleries and exedrae; however, the proportions of the Ravenna church are completely different: the arcades are extended much higher. A dome towers above them, brightly illuminated by eight windows.

The main structure, which has a quite simple exterior, is preceded by a vast atrium. The columns and capitals found in the interior were built in workshops in Constantinople. Valuable mosaic cycles have been preserved in the choir. In the center o[f] the vault we see the Lamb of God, a potent symbol of Christian triumph.

[A]bove and below: **Ravenna,** [S]. Vitale, 526–547, detail of the [m]osaic decoration in the choir: [t]he royal household of Emperor [J]ustinian; exterior view.

Opposite: **Ravenna,** S. Vitale, 526–547, view inside the octagon toward the northeast; the choir is on the right.

Istanbul, Hagia Sophia

"Solomon, I have surpassed thee!" The Byzantine emperor Justinian is said to have greeted the completion of Hagia Sophia with these words. In fact, the ruler could rightfully boast of having initiated a work that was at least on a par with the Biblical temple. The magnificent structure, with its central dome supported on four massive piers, was celebrated even by Justinian's contemporaries as "inexpressibly beautiful." The gold of the mosaics, the expansiveness of the interior—and not least, the revolutionary design of the dome, completely encircled with windows—cast a spell on viewers past and present.

Hagia Sophia was begun in 532 after an earlier building was destroyed in a revolt. The architects Anthemius of Tralles and Isidore of Miletus erected the church, whose typology includes elements of both centrally planned and basilical designs, over a period of just five years. Unfortunately, parts of the central dome collapsed in an earthquake in 558 and had to be rebuilt.

Opposite and above: **Istanbul,**
Hagia Sophia, Anthemius of Tralles
and Isidore of Miletus, 532–537,
overall view and view into the interior.

SACRED ARCHITECTURE OF THE CAROLINGIAN, OTTONIAN, AND ROMANESQUE PERIODS

The period between late antiquity and the high Middle Ages was long referred to as the "Dark Age," and in the past, the art produced between the Roman and Romanesque periods was often called "barbarian." Today, scholars recognize that the centuries between the fall of the Roman Empire and the realignment of Europe after the turn of the millennium represent an extremely fruitful era. What was once considered an interim period is now seen as an era of historical continuity, a bridge between the ancient world and the modern.

During this period, when the Western powers were realigning themselves and the Christian faith was being spread both by word of mouth and by force, sacred architecture began to function as a political signal. There were good reasons why Charlemagne let himself be crowned by Pope Leo III. Cathedrals and monasteries, palace chapels and parish churches swore an allegiance to both the Church and the empire.

Aachen's Palatine Chapel marks the magnificent beginning of a new era, in which the architectural and decorative ideals of antiquity and Early Christianity were resurrected. The imposing abbey churches of the Carolingian era were also symbols of regal entitlement. At the same time, their fortified westworks and crypts established the designs that would become obligatory throughout the coming centuries.

Following the collapse of the Carolingian Empire, the Salian, Ottonian, and Hohenstaufen rulers drew on the architectural style of the ninth century: the cathedrals of Speyer, Mainz, and Worms served as vehicles for the display of imperial power, and were built just as the

masons in France were beginning to experiment with the Gothic system of building. St Michael's church in Hildesheim was an important step toward subdividing and prioritizing the interior space of the church. Its modular system, which derives the ground plan from the measurements of the crossing square, laid the groundwork for the structural principles of Romanesque architecture.

This close relationship between clerical and secular also provoked opposition. At the monastery of Cluny in Burgundy, a movement arose among those who insisted that the pope should be recognized as the single spiritual authority. Three monasteries founded in quick succession by the Cluniac monks exerted a lasting French influence on later European sacred architecture, including the barrel vault and the rethinking of wall elevations. The pilgrimage churches that lined the route to Santiago de Compostela also experimented with the architectural forms developed at Cluny. In the twelfth century it was the Cistercians—and the ideal of austerity they promoted—that brought new impulses to medieval architecture.

At the same time, a wide variety of other developments were taking place. The knightly orders of Spain, for example, modeled their constructions on historic sites in the Holy Land; Byzantine forms made their way into the Western world via Venice; and in Tuscany, the preferred styles were marble facings and classicizing motifs. The Normans developed a distinctive monumental style that could be seen from Normandy to England, and even as far away as Sicily.

Above: **Kleinkomburg,** former abbey church of St Ägidius (St Giles), 12th century. This unadorned interior corresponds to current notions of a Romanesque church, but the fact is that many Romanesque churches were, at least in part, colorfully decorated.

Left: **S. Pere de Rodes,** former abbey church, 11th century, capital.

Opposite: **Vézelay,** former abbey church of Ste-Madeleine, main portal, 1125–1130. Many medieval churches are characterized by rich sculptural ornamentation. The tympanum at Vézelay depicts the miracle of Pentecost. At this period, it was more usual for churchgoers to be confronted with scenes of the Last Judgment, reminding them of God's omnipotence.

Pablo de la Riestra
A Typical Romanesque Church Building

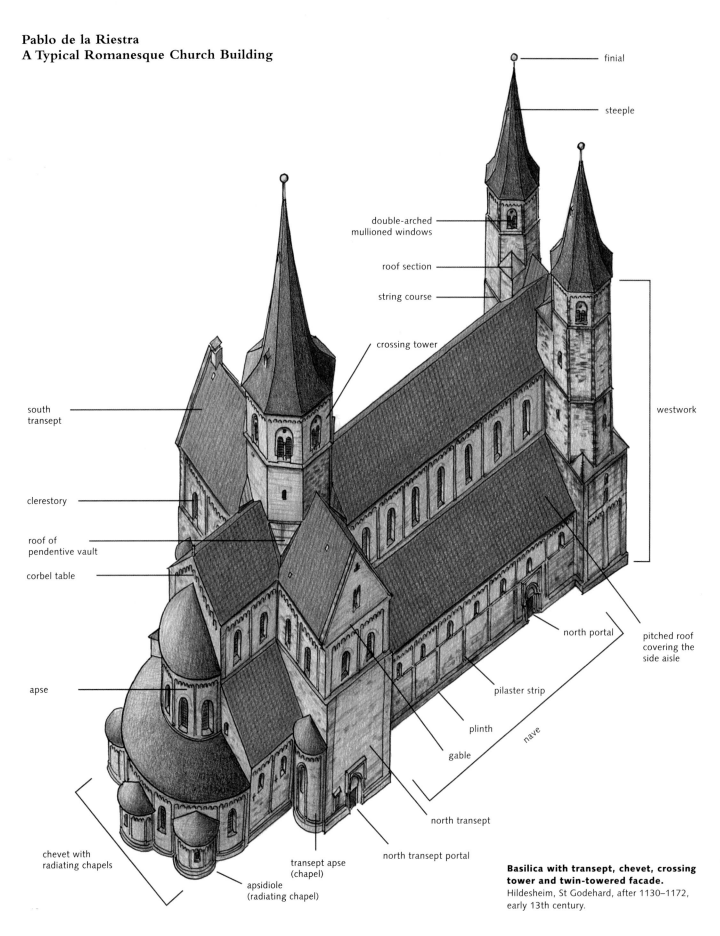

finial

steeple

double-arched mullioned windows

roof section

string course

crossing tower

westwork

south transept

clerestory

roof of pendentive vault

corbel table

apse

north portal

pitched roof covering the side aisle

pilaster strip

plinth

nave

gable

north transept

chevet with radiating chapels

transept apse (chapel)

north transept portal

apsidiole (radiating chapel)

Basilica with transept, chevet, crossing tower and twin-towered facade.
Hildesheim, St Godehard, after 1130–1172, early 13th century.

The Romanesque Church
Axonometric projection, floor plan, wall segment elevation

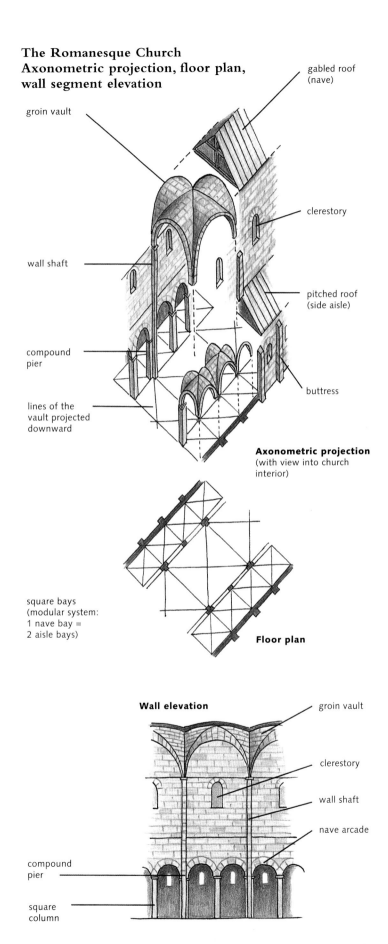

groin vault

gabled roof (nave)

clerestory

wall shaft

pitched roof (side aisle)

compound pier

buttress

lines of the vault projected downward

Axonometric projection
(with view into church interior)

square bays (modular system: 1 nave bay = 2 aisle bays)

Floor plan

Wall elevation

groin vault

clerestory

wall shaft

nave arcade

compound pier

square column

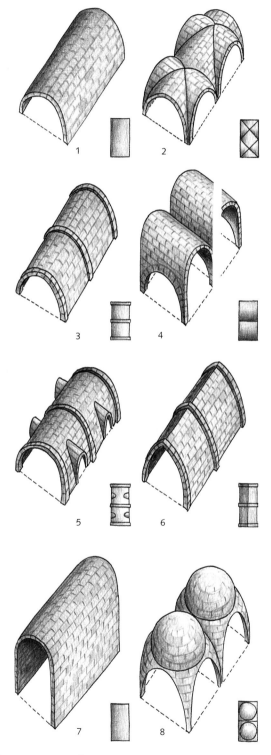

Romanesque vaults

1 barrel vault
2 groin vault
3 barrel vault with transverse arches
4 transverse barrel vaults

5 barrel vault with transverse arches and minor lateral vaults
6 pointed barrel vault with transverse arches
7 stilted barrel vault
8 domes with pendentives

Left: **Aachen,** Minster, former Palatine Chapel, dedicated 800; view of the interior of the octagon, which borrows motifs from S. Vitale in Ravenna.

Above: **Müstair,** Benedictine Convent of St John, ca. 800; view from the southeast, including the late Gothic bell tower and the abbess's tower.

Below: **Lorsch,** gatehouse to the atrium of the (destroyed) Abbey Church of St Nazarius, dedicated 774. The facade is decorated with antique spolia.

Carolingian Sacred Architecture

Charlemagne's coronation by Pope Leo III set the stage for significant changes in the way subsequent churches were constructed. Following the chaos of the migration period, during which few permanent sacred buildings were built, religious architecture dominated the next centuries, both in quantity and in quality. Church-building also assumed a more worldly role. Whereas previously, its main purpose had been to serve the cult of Christianity and pay tribute to the martyrs, it now took on increasingly political functions: palace, parish, and abbey churches—not to mention cathedrals—became testaments in stone to an empire that saw itself as the legitimate heir of the *Imperium Romanum*. Building techniques were formative in this: most buildings constructed in central Europe between the fifth and eighth centuries were non-vaulted wooden structures. Now, massive stone *more romano* construction effectively became the imperial style.

This twofold reference to the Roman Empire and the Roman Church served to reawaken the culture of antiquity. Church interiors were decorated with spoils from Rome and Ravenna, and late antique architectural and decorative forms inspired the design of the buildings.

The Palatine Chapel in Aachen represents the epitome of this Carolingian renaissance, and served as a prototype for countless medieval central-plan buildings. At its core is a domed octagon surrounded by a sixteen-sided, two-story gallery. The gatehouse of Lorsch recalls Roman triumphal arches, the elevation of the facade with columns and pilasters revealing an understanding of the classical orders.

Elements such as the Early Christian basilica with its longitudinal emphasis, the central plan with annexed areas, and the crypt (all of which were influenced by Roman imperial archi-

tecture) were adapted to fit new liturgical demands and clearly articulated in spatial terms. One striking example of this is the Benedictine Convent of St John in Müstair (Graubünden, Switzerland), which was founded by Charlemagne. The single-aisled church with its three apses was probably modeled on Byzantine interiors. In 1896, restoration work at the church revealed the most important surviving fresco cycle from ca. 800.

The monumental westwork flanked by two towers is believed to be a Carolingian invention. The most impressive surviving example is the former Abbey Church of Corvey. An integral element of this fortress-like structure, which is located at the entrance to the nave, is a two-story chapel set above the entrance hall.

Above left and right: **Corvey,** former abbey church, westwork, 873–885, chapel with surrounding gallery and facade.

This Carolingian westwork is the only one of its kind that survives almost completely unchanged.

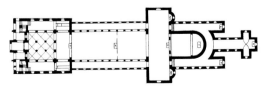

Carolingian Crypts

Great significance was attached to the crypt during the Carolingian period. Usually located beneath the high altar of the church, these places of worship housed the remains of Christian martyrs and saints from whom the faithful hoped to be endowed with healing and miracles.

The crypt evolved from the late antique *confessio*, an accessible martyr's tomb located in the eastern section of a church. The model for this structure was Old St Peter's in Rome, which contained the grave of the apostle Peter, one of the most venerated memorials in Christendom. During the Carolingian period, crypts were usually constructed in a tunnel or ring shape. Later, vast hall crypts were the preferred form, often with several aisles and imposing arrangements of columns. Crypts contained separate altars and provided enough space for large numbers of pilgrims to assemble for worship and prayer.

Above: **Steinbach,** former abbey church, known as Einhard's Basilica, 827. The crypt contains the remains of Roman saints.

Opposite: **Fulda,** St Michael, crypt, 820–822, built under Abbot Eigil; the monk Racholf is thought to have been the master builder.

Steinbach, Einhard's Basilica

Above: **Constance,** Minster of Our Lady, crypt, before 904.

Ottonian and Salian Church Architecture

Between 919 and 1024, rulers of the Ottonian dynasty controlled the Holy Roman Empire, followed by the Salians until 1125. Both these imperial houses, like the Carolingians before them, employed architecture in the service of regal representation, and its appearance clearly followed the traditions of their predecessors. Nevertheless, both floor plans and elevations were subjected to new, stricter forms of grouping and organization. The nave and transept were closely interrelated; the tower groupings on the west end were mirrored by towers on the eastern side; a massive crossing tower was often included as well. A western choir was frequently placed in opposition to the eastern choir. Church interiors were organized by the modular system (the base unit supplied by the crossing square) and articulated with alternating major and minor piers. The galleried church at Gernrode is the oldest example of this consistent division of space, while St Michael's at Hildesheim represents its crowning achievement. This Benedictine monastery church was begun in 1010 by Bishop Bernward and dedicated in 1033. Its unique painted wooden ceiling was added in the thirteenth century. The foundations of Romanesque art were laid in the tenth and especially eleventh centuries, and thus one often speaks in terms of the preromanesque or early Romanesque periods.

Opposite: **Gernrode,** St Cyriacus, interior. The alternation of major and minor piers divides the nave in a rhythmic pattern; the galleries on the upper level are modeled on Byzantine examples.

Right: **Gernrode,** former convent church of St Cyriacus, last third 10th century, view from the northwest (the apse dates from the 12th c.).

Below: **Hildesheim,** St Michael, 1010–1033, renovated after a fire 1162–1186, exterior view.

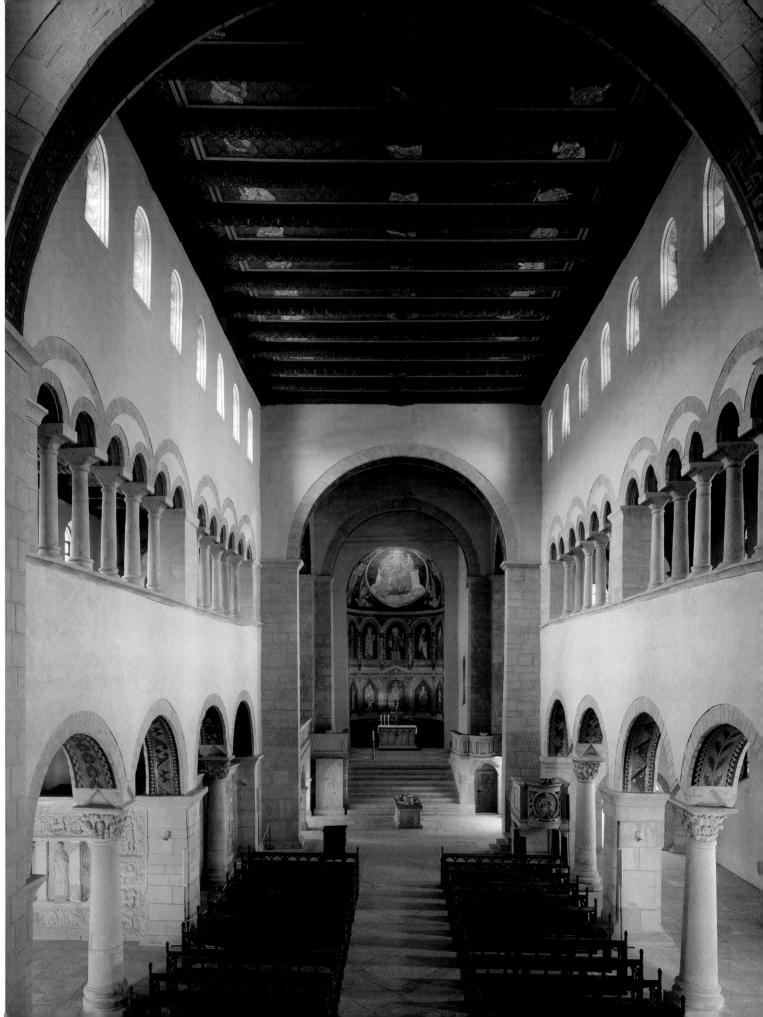

Above: **Trier,** Cathedral of St Peter, westwork, 1028. The imposing tower front, articulated with pilaster strips and corbel tables, is part of the renovation work initiated on this late antique building complex by Archbishop Poppo. The dwarf galleries above the portals are among the first of their kind.

Opposite: **Cologne,** St Pantaleon, westwork, 984–ca. 1000, reconstructed 1888–1892 after many changes. The exterior of this towering westwork is characterized by block shapes: the uncompromisingly square center tower is dwarfed by facetted side towers.

Speyer, Cathedral of St Mary and St Steven, 1030–1061 and 1082–1106, view from the southwest (above).
Right: detail of the exterior from the northwest. The nave walls and windows date from the first building phase; the transept and dwarf galleries were completed during the second phase.
Far right: south side aisle.

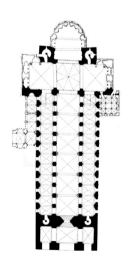

Speyer Cathedral

Speyer was one of the most important cities of the medieval Holy Roman Empire. As early as the tenth century, Salian counts sought to be buried there. After they ascended to the German kingship, Conrad II ordered the rebuilding of the bishop's church of St Mary and St Steven. This Romanesque basilica, which replaced older buildings, was intended to serve as the burial place of German kings and emperors for centuries to come. The majority of the construction took place in two phases. The cross-shaped main complex, including the vast nave, the transept, and the tower groupings, was completed during the first stage between 1030 and 1061 ("Speyer I"). From 1082 to ca. 1106, the new building ("Speyer II") was established: the crypt, crossing piers, and nave all received attention. The nave was heightened and vaulted, and a new, sculptural articulation sheathed the walls to help support the vaulted roof.

Speyer, cathedral, crypt, dedicated 1041. The hall crypt is the oldest section of the cathedral. The groin vault ceiling is supported by sturdy columns with cushion capitals.

The Imperial Cathedrals of Worms and Mainz

With its enormous scale and impressive vaulting, Speyer Cathedral served as a prototype for further imperial buildings, including the cathedrals of Mainz and Worms. In Mainz, Emperor Henry IV ordered the rebuilding of the Cathedral of St Martin and St Steven, which had been destroyed in a fire in 1081. The new structure was completed around 1137. Allusions to the older cathedral are especially evident in the eastern section: with the contrast between weight-bearing and non-supporting walls, the nave also repeats motifs found in Speyer. The Cathedral of Worms was rebuilt at the turn of the twelfth century over an Ottonian floor plan. Its western choir is composed of familiar stone blocks, but their design is more sculptural than those of earlier buildings.

Above, above right and right: **Mainz,** Cathedral of St Martin and St Steven, begun 1081, dedicated 1137, view into the nave; view from the east; and detail of the apse including dwarf gallery.

Opposite: **Worms,** Cathedral of St Peter, west choir, late 12th to early 13th centuries, incorporating older building elements. The apse and the domed crossing tower are richly decorated.

Maria Laach

The Benedictine Abbey Church of Maria Laach (photo opposite) was under construction for nearly 150 years. The hall crypt, nave, and west choir were dedicated in 1156, although the choir towers were not yet completed. The paradise—a type of porch or atrium adjacent to the westwork—may not have been finished until sometime between 1220 and 1230. This long construction period necessarily had an impact on the cathedral's style; the transition from an emphatically cubic concept to a sculptural/decorative one is clearly visible. In the nave, the previously customary alternation of major and minor piers is absent for the first time.

Cologne, St Aposteln

St Aposteln (Church of the Holy Apostles, photo top right), like all the churches in Cologne, has a long history. The existing structure combines a piered basilica built around 1020–1030 with the triconch completed in the early thirteenth century. Along with Gross St Martin, St Maria im Kapitol, and St Georg, St Aposteln is the fourth and latest church of this type in the city. Unlike its predecessors, its tower group is distinguished by more balanced proportions and consistent structural organization. Tiers of blind arches and dwarf galleries provide horizontal accents.

Cologne, St Maria im Kapitol

The Convent Church of St Maria im Kapitol (photo right) is considered a milestone of Lower Rhineland architecture. Built in the mid-eleventh century, it replaced earlier buildings whose roots go back to the seventh century. The marriage of the longitudinal and central plans proved groundbreaking: at the eastern end of the three-aisled nave, the church features a triconch, or clover-leaf choir, encircled by the continuation of the vaulted side aisles. A vast hall crypt, dedicated in 1049, extends beneath the main structure. The westwork contains a gallery reserved for the nuns that opens onto the central aisle.

Ratzeburg, Cathedral

A shortage of natural stone led to a heyday for brick construction in the Baltic region throughout the Middle Ages. Since the structural properties of brick, fired and worked in layers, are completely different from quarry stones, the use of brick led to a distinct type of formal expression from the twelfth century onward. Ratzeburg Cathedral is among the earliest large buildings built in brick. Although its style is traditional, the church is captivating with its contrasting colors and elaborately decorated facade, including cornices, pilaster strips, and lace-like friezes.

Left: **Ratzeburg,** Cathedral of St Mary and St John the Evangelist, begun 1160–1170, completed ca. 1210.

Limburg an der Lahn, Cathedral

Limburg Cathedral, formerly the Abbey Church of St George and St Nicholas, is worth special attention for more than its picturesque location high above the rocky banks of the Lahn River. From a stylistic standpoint, the three-aisled galleried church with seven steeply looming towers represents a turning point between the late German Romanesque and the early Gothic architecture imported from France. While the older Rhineland traditions are still clearly recognizable in the church's floor plan and its compact exterior, the choir gallery with its flying buttresses, the segmentation of the wall surfaces, and above all, the four-tiered vertical layout of the interior walls reveal its northern French precursors. The present structure, which replaced a complex built in the ninth and tenth centuries, is thought to have been initiated after 1211 and was not fully completed at the time of its dedication in 1235. It created the preconditions for the evolution of the German Gothic movement, which had its beginnings at the Church of St Elizabeth in Marburg and the Liebfrauenkirche (Church of Our Lady) in Trier.

Right and opposite: **Limburg an der Lahn,** former convent church, now Limburg Cathedral, 1211–1235, interior and exterior views.

Milan, S. Ambrogio

The primarily Romanesque S. Ambrogio stands above the grave of late fourth-century martyrs Protasius and Gervasius. Construction of a new basilica began in the ninth century, and its current appearance dates from 1088 to 1128. The atrium in front of the church, surrounded by columned halls, draws on an Early Christian architectural style. This was a gathering place for pilgrims, who came to the fountain to be symbolically cleansed from the stain of their sins. Whether the ribbed vault of the nave had been built by 1117—making it an extremely early example of this style—is a matter of historical debate.

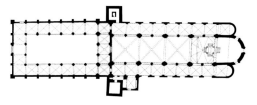

Opposite and top right: **Milan,** S. Ambrogio, 9th to 12th centuries, atrium and view into the nave facing east.

Below and below right: **Como,** S. Abbondio, dedicated 1095, view from the southwest and interior.

Como, S. Abbondio

As at S. Ambrogio in Milan, the building history of S. Abbondio in Como is largely uncertain. The Benedictine church is thought to have been started after 1063 and dedicated in 1095. The church's layout—with five aisles and without a transept—and its wood-covered roof truss are reminiscent of the Early Christian basilicas in Ravenna. The aisles are subdivided by drum piers with cushion capitals. The blocked in side apses are flanked by two towers, contributing to the blocky, somewhat austere character of the complex.

Verona, S. Zeno Maggiore

St Zeno, the miracle-working bishop and later patron saint of Verona, died in the year 380. No less than five sanctuaries were erected over his grave before building was begun in 1118 on the Romanesque church that still stands today. It was essentially completed in 1138, after only twenty years of construction. The majestic building is made of tuff and marble; inside, massive cruciform piers alternate with slender columns. At the eastern end of the nave, a partially sunken crypt extends across the entire width of the structure.

An outstanding feature of this church is the sculpted bronze portal doors, a creation of Maestro Niccolo and his workshop. In forty-six different panels, they depict the life and miracles of St Zeno.

Left: **Verona,** S. Zeno Maggiore, 1118–1138, view of the nave facing east. A monumental raised choir stands above the partially sunken crypt.

Venice, S. Marco

The Basilica of S. Marco in Venice contains the relics of St Mark the Evangelist, which were brought to Venice in 828–829. S. Marco represents a unique synthesis of Byzantine architecture and Venetian ornamental forms. Modeled after the Church of the Holy Apostles in Constantinople (sixth century), the five-domed structure built on a cross-shaped floor plan was begun in 1063, dedicated in 1073, and completed in 1094. The addition of its splendid decorations, which include gold mosaics, marble, and bronze, continued into the thirteenth century, making its construction a comprehensive work of medieval art.

Right and opposite: **Venice,** Basilica of S. Marco, begun 1063, facade facing St Mark's Square and view into the choir including late 12th-century mosaics

Modena, Cathedral

Initial construction of the Modena Cathedral began in 1099 under the direction of Countess Matilda of Tuscany. The three-aisled basilica with its magnificent silhouette is one of the major sacred buildings of the Emilia Romagna, in part because a wealth of information sur-vives about the artists involved in its construction. Master Lanfranco designed the building and Master Wiligelmus executed the sculptures on the facade. The cathedral was dedicated in 1184; it was remodeled several times between the thirteenth and fifteenth centuries.

Modena, Cathedral of S. Geminiano, begun 1099, dedicated 1184, facade with sculpture by Master Wiligelmus, early 12th century.

Parma, Cathedral and Baptistery

The center of Parma is dominated by the massive dimensions of the cathedral and campanile, the baptistery and the bishop's palace. The cornerstone for the cathedral was laid in the eleventh century under Bishop Cadalo. The further history of its construction is uncertain, since the city was devastated by an earthquake in 1117 that apparently caused heavy damage to the new structure. In 1281, Giambono da Bissone created the *protiro*, the porch with its two columns supported on lions. Work on the new campanile began shortly thereafter. The octagonal baptistery stands at the intersection between the Romanesque and Gothic styles. It is the work of Benedetto Antelami, who led construction between 1196 and 1216. Gifted in sculpture and architecture, Antelami also designed the three-dimensional design facade.

Right: **Parma,** baptistery, Benedetto Antelami and his assistants, 1196–1216, interior.

Below: **Parma,** Piazza del Duomo with cathedral, campanile, and baptistery, 11th to 13th centuries.

The Tuscan "Proto-Renaissance"

As early as the eleventh century, master builders in Tuscany were modeling their designs on the architecture of antiquity. Balanced proportions, the clear arrangement of surfaces, and the use of classical columns became the particular trademarks of the central Italian Romanesque style, which is also known as the "Proto-Renaissance." Narrow bands of light and dark marble in geometric patterns enliven the surfaces. This elaborate "encrustation" or inlay style endured well into the fifteenth century and decisive influenced the architecture of the Early Renaissance.

But the Tuscan builders certainly did not completely forego Romanesque decorative forms. The marble facade of Pisa Cathedral, for example, is intricately clad with a web-like arrangement of arcades and galleries, yet it emerges as structural clarity. A unique characteristic of the Pisan architectural style is the lozenge-shaped ornaments in the blind arches.

Opposite: **Florence,** S. Miniato al Monte, 1070–1093 (crypt and east section), 1128–1150 (west section and facade).

Below: **Pisa,** Campo dei Miracoli, cathedral, begun in 1063 under the direction of the architect Buscheto.

Right: **Florence,** Baptistery of St John, ca. 1060–1150. The octagonal structure is covered by a pavilion roof.

Apulia

The southern Italian province of Apulia is home to some unique examples of Romanesque architecture. It owes its cultural wealth to the Normans, who campaigned against the Byzantine and Arab hegemonies in the Mediterranean region.

With the foundation of S. Nicola in Bari, a uniquely Apulian architectural style was created that was copied in numerous churches along the Adriatic coast. Artistic preferences were not the only factor responsible for strong similarities between these structures. The mortal remains of St Nicholas of Myra, which had been seized by Barian sailors, transported to their homeland, and enshrined in the new church, were objects of greatest veneration in southern Italy. By imitating the architecture of S. Nicola, the cathedrals of Trani, Molfetta, Bitonto, Ruvo, and even Bari hoped to secure some of these relics' glamour for themselves.

Characteristic of this group of buildings are, among other things, the block-like continuous transept, the high central nave that towers above the side aisles and often features a large rose window on its facade, as well as the galleries and the open roof truss in the interior.

Opposite, top and bottom left: **Bari,**
S. Nicola, 1087–1196, interior and view
from the northwest. The church, sponsored by Roger I, incorporates elements
of an earlier Catapan palace (seat of the
Byzantine governor).

Opposite bottom right and above: **Trani,**
Cathedral of S. Nicola Pellegrino, late 11th
century. In competition with the church
in Bari, this cathedral was dedicated to
St Nicholas the Pilgrim. The massive transept features slender half-cylinder apses.

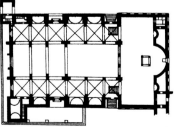

Bari, S. Nicola

Above: **Palermo,** cathedral, begun 1185, southern facade with its late Gothic main portal consisting of three wide, arched openings.

Right: **Monreale,** cathedral, mosaic decoration on the north wall depicting scenes from the Old Testament, late 12th to early 13th centuries.

Sicily

Sicily has been a cultural crossroads from time immemorial. After the Greeks and the Romans, the Arabs ruled over the island until 1072. They were followed by the Normans, who then merged with the Hohenstaufen dynasty. This medieval Norman-Hohenstaufen state was characterized by an extraordinarily fruitful coexistence of civilizations: classical, Byzantine, and Arab elements merged with western and central European traditions.

The Cathedral of Cefalù was founded by Roger II in 1131 and intended as a burial place for the Norman rulers; its construction was an impressive demonstration of imperial power. The cathedral's architecture reveals Anglo-Norman influences, while its Byzantine legacy can be found in many details, particularly in the mosaic decoration of the apse. The Cathedral of Monreale also holds a special status. Its Byzantine mosaics, Arab floor decoration, Pisan bronze doors, and the cloister with its fancifully designed capitals form a unique conglomerate of occidental and oriental art forms.

Below: **Cefalù,** view of the city from the west including the Norman cathedral. Its double-towered facade was completed in 1240.

Above: **Cefalù,** cathedral, 1131 to late 12th century, view into the apse. The mosaics in the apse date back to 1148 and are some of the oldest in Sicily.

Reims, St-Rémi

In the year 1005, Abbot Airard laid the corner-stone for the new Abbey Church of St-Rémi. With a length of 330 feet (100 m) and a transept width of almost 215 feet (65 m), it was intended to cover a vast expanse of space. Following the death of Airard in 1034, his successor began to scale the project back to a more modest size. Nevertheless, the layout of the nave suggests the design of an early Romanesque basilica: compound piers support the nave arcade, and equally wide gallery arches open above it. The new church was dedicated in 1049. Initially it had a flat roof; the church's Gothic appearance dates from 1170–1190.

Left: **Reims,** St-Rémi, begun 1005–1190, nave, section of the early Romanesque wall with Gothic modifications.

Tournus, St-Philibert

As with many medieval churches, the building history of the Abbey Church of St-Philibert in Tournus is difficult to reconstruct. Its imposing, three-aisled narthex is thought to have been built primarily during the tenth century, and the chapel of St Michael on the upper level probably dates from the eleventh century. The nave, which was apparently built around the same time, amazes visitors with its extraordinary height and hall-like breadth. Compact brick drum piers support transverse barrel vaults that rest on free-standing arches. This vaulting, which was most likely added after the building was complete, creates a fantastic sense of space. Nevertheless, it was never emulated in any significant structures.

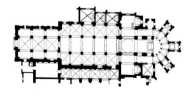

Left and opposite:
Tournus, St-Philibert, 10th to 12th centuries, view from the southeast, interior facing east.

Normandy

Normandy, the stretch of the French coast flanking the English Channel, took on a special status in Europe during the tenth, eleventh, and twelfth centuries. Under Norman rule, a stable political structure had developed there, and engaged in continual exchanges, both economic and cultural, with other regions. The Normans' dynastic relationships extended as far as Sicily, which developed a Norman culture of its own. The contact between the Normans and England—a country they conquered in the Battle of Hastings in 1066—was particularly close. In terms of architecture, therefore, one can justifiably speak of an Anglo-Norman style in this time period. Its unique features include twin-towered facades, galleries, double-shelled construction, and the vaulting of naves and transepts.

The former Abbey Church of St-Étienne (St Stephen) in Caen combines all of these characteristics. It was founded in 1066 by William the Conqueror and his consort Matilda, who hoped to thereby make amends to Rome for marrying each other in spite of a papal ban. Matilda had already sponsored the Convent Church of the Holy Trinity (Ste-Trinité, also in Caen) seven years earlier. William was buried in St-Étienne in 1087.

Caen, St-Étienne, begun 1066, vaulted 1100–1120, choir added ca. 1200; view into the nave with its wide gallery openings and view of the Gothic choir.

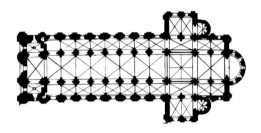

Both of these churches represent milestones in the history of architecture, despite the fact that they underwent numerous modifications over time. Among other things, a Gothic choir was added to St-Étienne around 1200.

The former Priory Church of St-Vigor in Cerisy-la-Forêt, on the other hand, was never vaulted, and its choir section was never expanded; it thus allows us to make inferences about the eastern side of St-Étienne. Cerisy establishes a link between the monastic churches in Caen and the Romanesque churches built in England after 1066.

Left: **Caen,** Ste-Trinité (Church of the Holy Trinity), 1059–1066 (crypt and nave), 1100–1130 (eastern section and vaulting). The massive, twin-towered facade is a typical feature of Norman architecture.

Below: **Cerisy-la-Forêt,** St-Vigor, ca. 1080/1085–ca. 1120. This former priory church still contains its original Romanesque choir. The western section was destroyed in the 19th century.

Toulouse, St-Sernin

Like Conques, St-Sernin in Toulouse is one of the five great pilgrimage churches along the route to Santiago de Compostela, or the Way of St James. In order to provide space for huge crowds of the faithful, they developed a very specific form: a projecting transept supplemented by apses and a chevet with apsidioles (choir with ambulatory and radiating chapels). With five aisles and eleven bays, the nave is immense in its proportions. The church, which is dedicated to St Saturnin, was begun in 1080 and completed around the middle of the twelfth century.

Opposite: **Toulouse,** St-Sernin, 1080 to mid-12th century; view of the transept and chevet; tower 12th to 13th centuries.

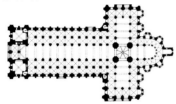

Conques, Ste-Foy

The Abbey Church of Ste-Foy in Conques was originally begun in a more modest, antiquated style. As the influx of pilgrims to the relics of the martyr multiplied, a more spacious apse was built, modeled on St-Sernin. The nave was given a barrel vault whose thrust was absorbed by galleries. Like all the churches on the Way of St James, Ste-Foy is richly decorated with sculpture. The tympanum on the western portal depicts the Last Judgment; with 124 figures, it is the most complex example surviving from the Romanesque period.

Top and right: **Conques,** Ste-Foy, tympanum and general view; building 1050–1130, sculpture 1135–1140.

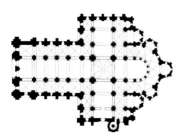

Autun, St-Lazare, 1120 to mid-12th century. The cathedral once contained the tomb of St Lazarus, whose relics were transferred here with great ceremony in 1146; a bitter dispute later broke out over these remains.
The figurative capitals inside the church are among the most beautiful of that period (today they are displayed in the Chapter House Museum). Pictured here are Flight into Egypt and the Suicide of Judas, 1120–1130.

Autun, Cathedral of St-Lazare

The master builder of Autun Cathedral, Bishop Étienne Bâgé, was a fervent supporter of the Cluniac church reforms. It is thus no surprise that his church drew much of its inspiration from the third Abbey Church of Cluny, built between 1088 and 1130. This is particularly evident in the harmonization and unity of the building elements and the division of the levels. Classical elements were neatly integrated into the Romanesque system. Fluted pilasters lend a rhythmic structure to the walls, and the string courses are adorned with bead moldings and rosette friezes. The blind arches of the triforium are modeled after the Roman city gates that can still be seen in Autun today.

St-Lazare is particularly captivating for its wealth of sculpture. The portal complex, created by Master Gislebertus around 1130, is one of the masterpieces of Romanesque sculpture in existence. Marvelous capitals inside the church featuring Old and New Testament scenes have been preserved; some of these are also the work of Gislebertus.

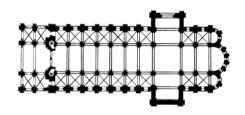

Opposite: **Autun,** Cathedral of St-Lazare, western portal, ca. 1130; the tympanum depicting the Last Judgment is the work of the master sculptor Gislebertus.

Cluny, Paray-le-Monial, and Vézelay

In 910, William of Aquitaine founded a Benedictine monastery in the Burgundian town of Cluny that came to epitomize monastic reform and self-governance. The Cluniac monks recognized papal authority alone, not that of any secular ruler. Their ideas met with widespread approval, and their architecture was equally influential. The second (955–981) and third (1088–1130) churches, especially, which were constructed in quick succession, set new standards for European sacred architecture. Since Cluny III was destroyed in 1790, its size and splendor can only be appreciated based on the buildings it inspired. The priory church at Paray-le-Monial, for example, with its narthex, pointed arch vaults, and staggered chevet, is thought to be a miniature replica of the earlier structure.

In contrast, after its Carolingian nave was destroyed by fire in 1120, St Mary Magdalene in Vézelay was outfitted with groin vaults. The transverse arches supporting them were accented in two colors, emphasizing the aisle's extraordinary feeling of spaciousness.

Opposite: **Vézelay,** Ste-Madeleine, ca. 1120–1150, view into the nave with two-tiered wall elevation and classicizing decoration.

Above: **Cluny III,** view from the east in the 16th century. This lithograph dates from after 1789, Paris, Bibliothèque Nationale, cabinet des Estampes.

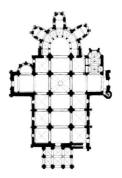

Left and above: **Paray-le-Monial,** priory church, ca. 1100, view from the northeast; interior view toward the east; floor plan.

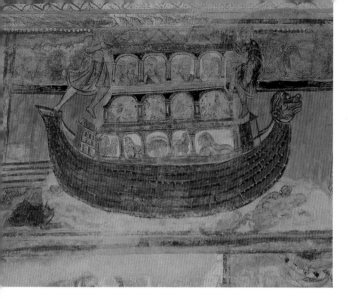

Western France

The sacred architecture of western France pursued a different course than that in Burgundy—which was strongly influenced by Cluniac ideas—or the galleried churches of Normandy. In Aquitaine and Poitou the preferred forms were hall churches with barrel vaults or rib vaults, or domed churches with nave bays that were vaulted with a series of pendentive domes. The first type is exemplified by the former Abbey Church of St-Savin-sur-Gartempe, whose nave was built between 1095 and 1115. Its aisles are separated by elegant columned arcades, and the barrel vault extends through the nave with no transverse arches. The vault was built without direct light; instead, it features one of the most detailed mural cycles in France. Its thirty-six pictures narrate the story of Creation, the life of Noah, the Great Flood, and more. The paintings were added near the end of the eleventh century.

The cathedrals of Angoulême and Périgueux represent the domed type of church. The former was built in the shape of a Latin cross, the latter in that of a Greek cross. Their square bays are topped by four and five domes respectively, which rest on sloping spandrels (pendentives). It is quite possible that this type of vaulted roof was inspired by Early Christian or Byzantine examples; the Cathedral of S. Marco in Venice may also have been their immediate prototype.

St-Savin-sur-Gartempe,
1060–1085 (eastern section) and
1095–1115 (renovation of the
nave); ceiling fresco depicting
Noah's Ark (above left) and nave
(left and above right).

Left: **Périgueux**, Cathedral of St-Front, initial construction after 1120. The exterior of the five-domed church was radically reconstructed in the 19th century.

Below right: **Angoulême,** Cathedral of St-Pierre, 12th century. The west facade, built between 1115 und 1136, contains one of the most complex sculptural programs of the French Romanesque period. It depicts scenes from the History of Salvation and from the Song of Roland.

Below: **Fontevraud,** former abbey church, founded in 1110. At the end of the 12th century, the domed church served as a burial site for the royal house of Plantagenet.

The Cistercians

At the outset of the twelfth century, discontent arose over the expansion of Cluniac wealth and power. The unrest culminated in the founding of the Cistercian Order, in 1098, a monastic movement that promised to return to the original rule established by St Benedict. Religious devotion, labor, and austerity were the values stipulated by the most famous Cistercian abbot, Bernhard of Clairvaux. Cistercian architecture was designed to embody these ideals. The Abbey of Cîteaux was the first monastery Bernard founded; it was followed by La Ferté, Pontigny, Morimond, and Clairvaux. These, in turn, quickly founded daughter houses. All the Cistercian monasteries followed the same ideal plan, which specified the overall layout of the abbey as well as the details of its furnishings.

Fontenay, abbey church, 1139–1147, view of the dormitory and church; interior of the church; and plan of the monastery.

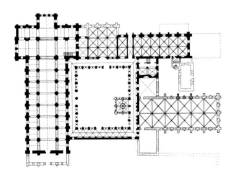

Pontigny and Fontenay

Of all the early Cistercian monasteries, only Fontenay, the second daughter house of Clairvaux, has preserved its original appearance—most likely dictated by Bernard himself. The church interior, constructed between 1139 and 1147, is notable for its sublime austerity. There are no superfluous architectural or decorative details; the exquisite masonry work is the church's one and only ornament. Pointed barrel vaults cover the nave and transept; the chapels on the east side are enclosed by sheer walls. Light enters the building only through the wall of the triumphal arch above the main choir.

Pontigny was founded as early as 1114, the direct daughter house of Cîteaux Abbey, but it was radically redesigned in the second half of the twelfth century. Among other things, a polygonal Gothic choir was added to the 350-foot (108-m) long building. Nevertheless, we can still recognize Bernhard's ideals in the unadorned nave. It is interesting to note that bell towers were never added to any Cistercian churches, since even these were considered ornamental. At most, a simple ridge turret would house the bell that called the monks to prayer.

Pontigny, abbey church, begun 1145, choir 1186–1210. The Romanesque nave and early Gothic choir are distinguished by their simplicity and clarity.

1

Romanesque architectural sculpture

With very few exceptions, Romanesque building sculpture is very closely linked to the architecture itself. Unlike the freestanding sculpture of antiquity, it is usually in the form of a relief or is subordinate to the architectural structure. The sculpture can thus be seen as an intermediate art form between purely two-dimensional painting and spatial, three-dimensional sculpture. The most prominent setting for sculpture on the exterior of a church is the portal; in the interiors, it primarily decorates capitals and corbels. As a form of architectural ornamentation, its role is purely decorative; architectural sculpture is figurative in character.

Portal sculpture

The precursors of richly sculptured portals such as that at Vézelay (p. 18) can be seen at left (1–3). Above the simple, early Romanesque door lintel (Fig. 1), which was particularly well suited for depicting a row of figures, the arched tympanum quickly took shape. From the late eleventh to the early fourteenth centuries, this became a central location for figurative imagery. Fig. 2 shows a typical early motif, Christ as *Maiestas Domini* in the mandorla, flanked by angels. In Fig. 3, the structure has become bizonal: the tympanum is separated from the architrave by means of an ornamental string course whose form

1 **St-Genis-des-Fontaines,** door lintel, 1019–1020.

2 **Charlieu,** former Priory Church of St Fortunatus, tympanum of the west portal, late 11th century.

3 **Toulouse,** St-Sernin, tympanum of the *Porte Miégeville*, before 1118.

4 **Aulnay-de-Saintonge,** former Collegiate Church St-Pierre-de-la-Tour, tympanum of the south portal, after 1130.

5 **Semur-en-Brionnais,** former Priory Church of St-Hilaire, west portal, secon half of the 12th century.

6 **Freiberg,** *Goldene Pforte*, ca. 1230.

2

3

4

5

6

7

8

9

suggests a row of clouds. Fig. 4, more or less contemporary with Vézelay, clearly demonstrates the extent to which regionally influenced differences (in this case, between Burgundian and western French architectural sculpture) can manifest themselves. Fig. 5 is later than Vézelay and already illustrates progressive development of the nested arches that would be typical for Gothic church portals. In the *Goldene Pforte* (Golden Gate) of Freiberg Cathedral (Fig. 6), the apogee of Romanesque portal sculpture in Germany, the arches are richly decorated with archivolt figures. Here, a design element that had already been seen on numerous portals in France appeared in Germany for the first time.

Capital sculpture

The column, a favorite supporting element since antiquity, consists of a base, a shaft, and a capital. Their organization is reminiscent of trees or plants, which may have been the model for their construction. The intermediate element between the support and the load is the capital, the "head" of the column; from both a constructional and a symbolic standpoint, it is a junction point in the structure. The Romanesque period introduced new types of capitals that arose independently of any classical models. These were the abstract block or cushion capital and the figuratively decorated "historiated" capital, which featured allegorical images and scenes from the Gospels. The examples shown here clearly trace the development from primarily material and structurally-determined forms to venues for complex programs of images (7–12).

7 **Cologne,** St-Maria im Kapitol, cushion capital, mid-11th century.

8 **Quedlinburg,** St Servatius, block capital with figurative ornamentation, before 1129.

9 **Serrabone,** Notre-Dame, double capital of the choir gallery, second half of the 12th century.

10 **Dijon,** rotunda of the Abbey Church of St-Benigne, historiated capital, early 11th century.

11 **Moissac,** Abbey Church of St-Pierre, historiated capital in the cloister, ca. 1100.

12 **S. Domingo de Silos,** double capitals in the cloister, mid-12th century.

10

11

12

La Seu d'Urgell

The imposing Cathedral of La Seu d'Urgell in the Pyrenees Mountains is the third structure to be erected at this location. Its cornerstone was laid sometime between 1116 und 1122. The work only moved forward, however, near the end of the century, when the Italian master builder Raimundus Lambardus was commissioned to lead the project. He brought elements of northern Italian architecture with him to Catalonia.

Cardona

The castle church of St Vicenç was financed by Viscount Beremund and constructed between 1029 and 1040. It is considered to be one of the milestones of Catalonian Romanesque architecture. Lombard workshops may also have made a contribution, but the regional traditions are dominant. The interior is completely vaulted, and the crossing is topped by an octagonal squinch cupola. The walls were articulated with an innovative graduated relief.

La Seu d'Urgell, cathedral, begun between1116 and 1122, eastern section. The apse, with its engaged columns and dwarf gallery, is reminiscent of northern Italian prototypes.

Above and opposite: **Cardona,** St Vicenç, 1029–1040, view of the castle mount and church from the northeast; interior view. The church's nave, choir, and transept arms are covered with barrel vaults.

Santiago de Compostela, Cathedral

Since the tenth century, Santiago de Compostela, the reputed gravesite of St James the Apostle, has been the destination for endless streams of pilgrims. In approximately 1075, the cornerstone was laid here for one of the mightiest Romanesque cathedrals. The highlight of its design is the magnificent west portal, the *Portico de la Gloria*, built by Master Mateo. Its trumeau depicts the Apostle James; above it is Christ in Majesty presiding over the Last Judgment. Built between 1168 and 1188, it is now protected by an equally elaborate baroque porch.

Frómista, S. Martín

One of the most important stations along the Pilgrims' Way is S. Martín in Frómista, construction of which may have begun even before 1066. The compact building, flanked by round towers, is famous for its unique capitals and corbels as well as its exquisite stonemasonry.

Opposite: **Santiago de Compostela,** Cathedral, west portal (*Pórtico de la Gloria*), the work of Master Mateo, last third of the 12th century.

Right and below: **Frómista,** Church of S. Martín, founded 1066(?) to after 1100, view of the exterior from the southwest showing flanking towers.

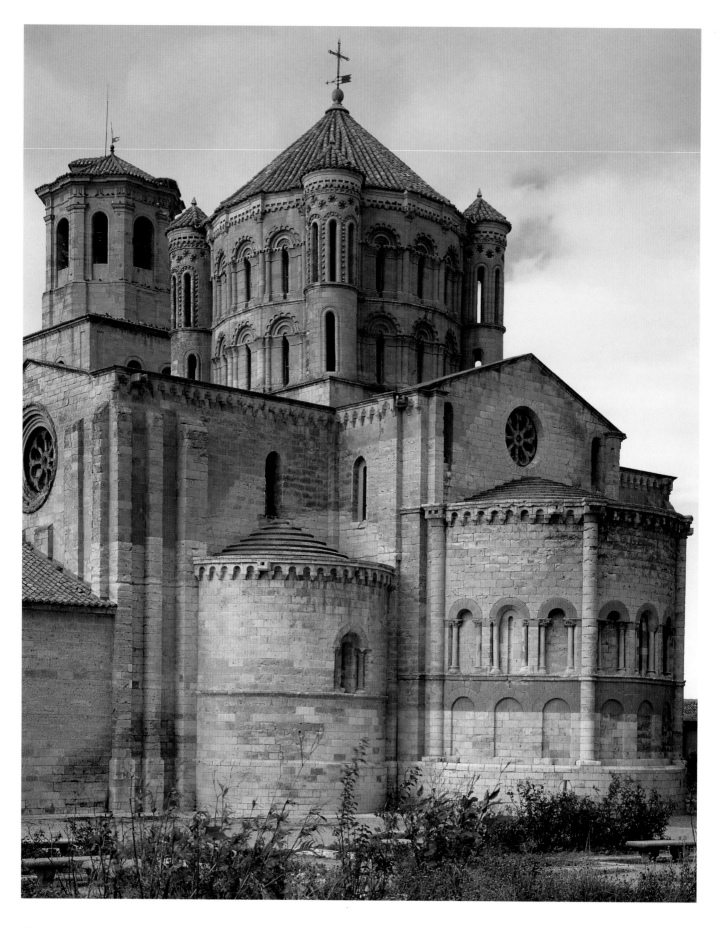

The Spanish Cimborrios

Unique to Spanish sacred architecture are the Romanesque *cimborrios*, monumental umbrella-shaped domes that rise above the crossing of the worship space. The vault, divided by ribs into sixteen sections, rests on a window-filled drum, which in turn is supported on pendentives. Some magnificent examples of this architectural element—otherwise unknown in European Romanesque building—are the cimborrios at Zamora Cathedral (1151–1171) and the Old Cathedral in Salamanca (1152 to the early thirteenth century), as well as at the Collegiate Church in Toro (begun 1160). They may well have been inspired by north African buildings such as the *mihrab* of the Great Mosque in Kairouan, or the Dome of the Rock in Jerusalem. The exterior appearance of the cimborrio is also quite idiosyncratic: turret porches cluster round the drum, lending it a bizarre character. However, these also serve a structural purpose by supporting the crossing tower and receive the thrust of the dome.

Opposite: **Toro,** Collegiate Church of S. María la Mayor, 1160–1240, view from the south with the cimborrio, transept, and apses.

Above and below: **Zamora,** cathedral, 1151–1171, view from the southwest; view into the cimborrio. This church served as a prototype for the domes in Toro and Salamanca.

Above left and right: **Tomar,** Templar Church, late 12th century, exterior and interior views. Construction of this church may have begun in 1187, when Jerusalem was conquered by the Arabs.

Below: **Segovia,** Iglesia de la Vera Cruz, dedicated 1208. The Church of the True Cross is thought to have been built by the Order of Canons of the Holy Sepulcher.

The Central-Plan Buildings of the Knightly Orders

The Spanish and Portuguese knightly orders played an important role in the *Reconquista*, the Christian recapture of power in Spain. In addition, with their buildings, which were frequently modeled after historic sites in the Holy Land, they ushered in a process of internationalization in architecture, which had previously been dominated by regional or French styles.

The Templar Church in the Portuguese city of Tomar was most likely intended to be a replica of the Church of the Holy Sepulcher in Jerusalem. The exterior of the Charola (or rotunda) is a sixteen-sided polygon; inside it is a freestanding octagonal chapel. The Church of the True Cross in Segovia has a similar plan, although this structure is twelve-sided, with three apses added to the east and an embrasured portal on the west, giving the central plan a longitudinal axis. The church is vaulted with a small dome, supported on parallel flat, load-bearing ribs.

Coimbra, Sé Velha (Old Cathedral)

With its compact walls, embrasured windows, and defiant crown of battlements, the Sé Velha (or Old Cathedral) in Coimbra has a fortress-like character. Construction of the Sé Velha was begun in 1140, one year after Afonso Henriques assumed the throne as the first king of Portugal and declared Coimbra the capital city of his realm. The building was completed in 1180, and it served as the Coronation Church until 1260, when the royal residence was transferred to Lisbon. The cathedral's interior, with its galleries, barrel vault, and transept, clearly shows the influence of the churches along the Pilgrims' Way.

Coimbra, Sé Velha (Old Cathedral), 1140–1180, view into the south transept and nave; exterior views of the west facade and the choir.

Ely, Cathedral

The history of the Benedictine Abbey of Ely goes back to the seventh century. The present church was begun in 1083 by Simeon, the first Norman abbot; it was elevated to the rank of cathedral in 1109. The three-aisled nave with thirteen bays is enormous in scale; however, its proportions are not atypical of Anglo-Norman architecture. After the crossing tower collapsed in a fire in 1322, it was replaced by a massive octagon, an extraordinary, 400-ton wooden structure whose exterior was encased in lead. The ceiling frescoes in the nave date from the nineteenth century.

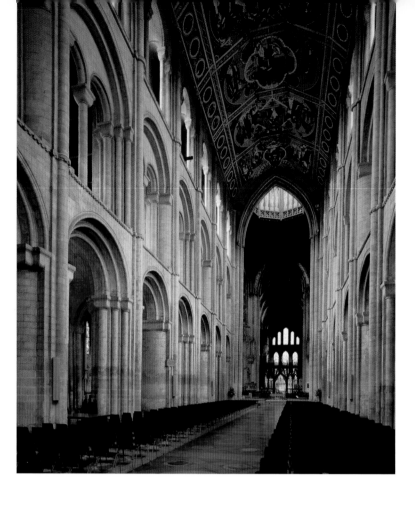

Right and opposite: **Ely,** cathedral, begun 1083, completed during the first half of the 12th century. The octagon was constructed of wood between 1322 and 1342, based on a design by Sexton Alan of Welsingham.

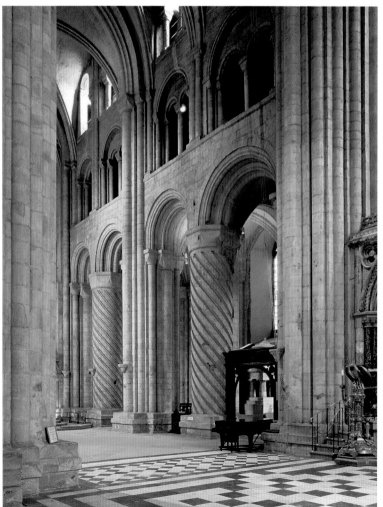

Durham, Cathedral

Durham Cathedral is among the most impressive examples of Anglo-Norman architecture. Situated high above the banks of the River Wear, its imposing exterior demonstrates the enormous ecclesiastical and secular power of the Norman rulers.

Like their counterparts on the French mainland, builders here also experimented with stone vaulting. When construction of the cathedral began in 1093, this technique had apparently already been planned for the choir; the rib vaults used for the entire nave—thought to be the earliest of their kind—were built in a second phase of construction that began around 1120. The most characteristic feature of the nave elevation is the striking alternation of compound piers and massive drum piers.

Left: **Durham,** cathedral, 1093–1133; west end ca. 1175; the west towers were constructed and the choir redesigned in the 13th century.

Norwich, Cathedral

In 1091, Herbert de Losinga, the former prior of Fécamp Abbey in Normandy, founded the Cathedral of the Holy Trinity in Norwich. The choir and the two side aisles were constructed first; work on the fourteen-bayed, three-tiered nave continued into the mid-twelfth century. The original plans for the nave apparently included a simple wooden roof; the decorative late Gothic fan vaults were installed in the fourteenth and fifteenth centuries. The present spire, which soars 315 feet (96 m) into the air, also dates from the fourteenth century.

Norwich, Cathedral of the Holy Trinity, begun 1091; work was completed in the 14th and 15th centuries; interior (below) and exterior view with crossing tower.

Cistercian Churches in England

As elsewhere in Europe, Cistercian abbeys in England were modeled on the ideals that evolved under Bernhard of Clairvaux. Thanks to the system of filiation (the strictly organized founding of daughter houses) the model of the original French abbeys was passed on repeatedly, even to the point of including their regional—in this case, usually Burgundian—stylistic elements. The architecture was also adjusted to meet with the local conditions, for example, in the choice of building materials.

Unfortunately, over the course of centuries, most of the Cistercian abbeys in England were destroyed—as in the case of Fountains Abbey and Rievaulx Abbey (both in Yorkshire), which today stand as exquisitely picturesque ruins.

Left: **Fountains Abbey,** former
Cistercian abbey, founded in
1135, view of the church ruins.

Below: **Rievaulx Abbey,** former
Cistercian abbey, founded in 1132,
view of the church and remains of
the monastery.

Lund, Cathedral

The Scandinavian countries embraced Christianity relatively late, between the ninth and the twelfth centuries. The oldest churches there were built of wood or field stones; the first monumental dressed stone buildings appeared in the eleventh century. Among these is the imposing Lund Cathedral, which was dedicated in 1145. This three-aisled, vaulted basilica is richly ornamented. Its style follows in the tradition of the Speyer Cathedral.

Borgund, Stave Church

In Scandinavia, wood was long the preferred building material. In Norway, approximately thirty stave churches still testify to the skilled craftsmanship of medieval carvers and carpenters. Their walls are constructed with posts, forming a wooden skeleton, and the roofs overlap in tiers. An impressive late example of this architecture is the church in Borgund, which dates from the mid-twelfth century.

Below left and right: **Lund,** cathedral, ca. 1104–1145, restored in the 19th century. Lund Cathedral was built of light-colored sandstone.

Right and opposite: **Borgund,** stave church, ca. 1150. Borgund is considered the most sophisticated of the thirty or so surviving stave churches in Norway.

THE GOTHIC PERIOD

In the fifteenth and sixteenth centuries, Italian art theorists described everything they considered cloddish and barbaric as *maniera dei goti* (in the manner of the Goths). These Renaissance writers, who wished to revive the heritage of classical architecture, saw the medieval art of northern Europe, in particular, as inferior in quality. Only in the late eighteenth and early nineteenth centuries, when Romantics rediscovered the architecture of the pre-Renaissance period, was a generally positive opinion of this era reestablished.

Today, the art of the late Middle Ages—from approximately the second half of the twelfth century to the early sixteenth century—is referred to as Gothic, although its development differed from region to region. The first elements of Gothic stylistic forms appeared as early as 1140 in France, but the transition from late Romanesque to early Gothic styles did not occur in Germany until the thirteenth century. Attempts to pinpoint the end of this stylistic era meet with the same problem: at the same time Michelangelo was bringing Renaissance architecture to full bloom in Italy, bold late Gothic hall churches were still being built elsewhere.

The definition of Gothic in architecture thus has less to do with date than with constructional details such as pointed arches and rib vaults. These in turn are part of an overall aesthetic concept whose goal was the dissolution of walls and the saturation of space with light. This dematerialization is more than just formal; it puts into practice the mystical ideals developed in literature and philosophy of that period. At the same time, the establishment of the Gothic style in France is closely connected to consolidation of the monarchy. The sacred buildings that definitively characterized the genre were all intimately connected with the court: the Abbey Church of St-Denis, intended as a burial site for French royalty; the Coronation Cathedral of Reims or the palace chapel in Paris, the Sainte-Chapelle. Gothic architecture became a prestige symbol, and a veritable competition arose between builders at Reims, Chartres, and Amiens. Each sought to construct the largest, most beautiful, most technically sophisticated building. Only the spectacular collapse of the choir at Beauvais Cathedral in 1284 brought the building frenzy to an end.

The reformed monastic orders played a significant role in the internationalization of the Gothic style. Through the Cistercians, whose ideal plan was passed on nearly unchanged from one abbey to another, the Gothic ideas of formal design made inroads throughout Europe. They were adapted to suit local traditions, for example, the brick structures of the Baltic region developed their own charming aesthetic.

The essence of Gothic architecture is the skeletal system, which allows wide, high spaces to be vaulted without significant reinforcement of the foundation walls. Instead, flying buttresses and abutments divert the thrust of vaults constructed between ribs, and the pressure of walls pierced with windows, toward the outside of the structure (*see* Chartres, pp. 90–91, and Coutances, p. 100).

A Gothic interior resembles a glass shrine, outlined by the delicate structure of its organizational elements. Builders in Normandy first developed the double-shelled system: while the inner layer was broken up by arcades, engaged columns, and wall moldings, the outer shell appears to be a mere membrane. Tracery, a type of architectural ornamentation derived from basic geometric elements, subdivided windows and later wall surfaces. By the late Gothic period, a system of relatively simple forms had developed into a dizzying net of lines. The same phenomenon occurred with the vaults, which became an experimental field for bold and extravagant construction.

Above: **Lübeck,** Marienkirche (Church of St Mary), vault of the Annenkapelle (Chapel of St Anne, also called the Epistle Chapel).

Left: **Salem,** former Cistercian abbey church, detail of a tracery window.

Opposite: **Carcassonne,** Cathedral of St-Nazaire, view into the choir and transept, begun ca. 1280. Its daring construction could only be accomplished with the help of visible tension bars.

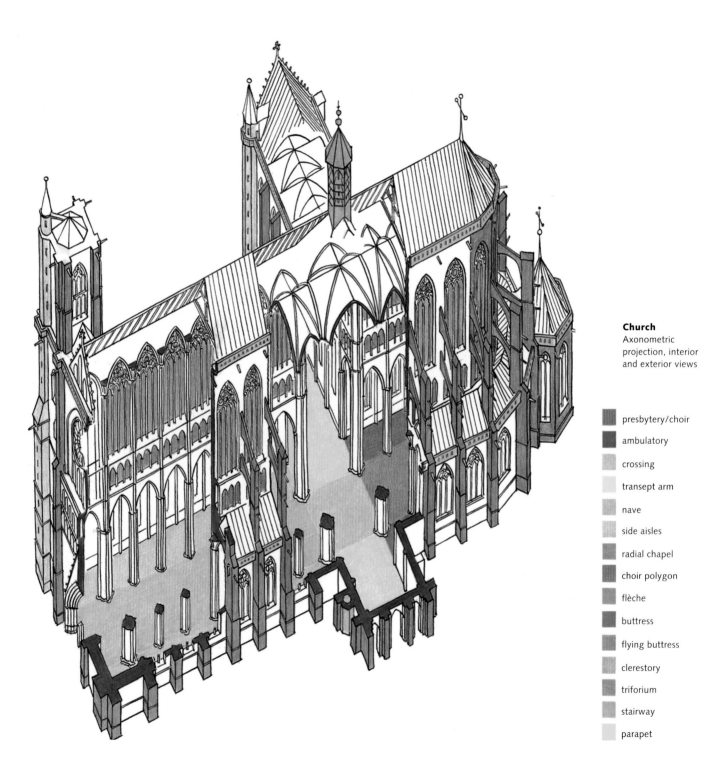

Church
Axonometric
projection, interior
and exterior views

- presbytery/choir
- ambulatory
- crossing
- transept arm
- nave
- side aisles
- radial chapel
- choir polygon
- flèche
- buttress
- flying buttress
- clerestory
- triforium
- stairway
- parapet

The Gothic Basilica
Axonometric projection,
floor plan, wall elevation

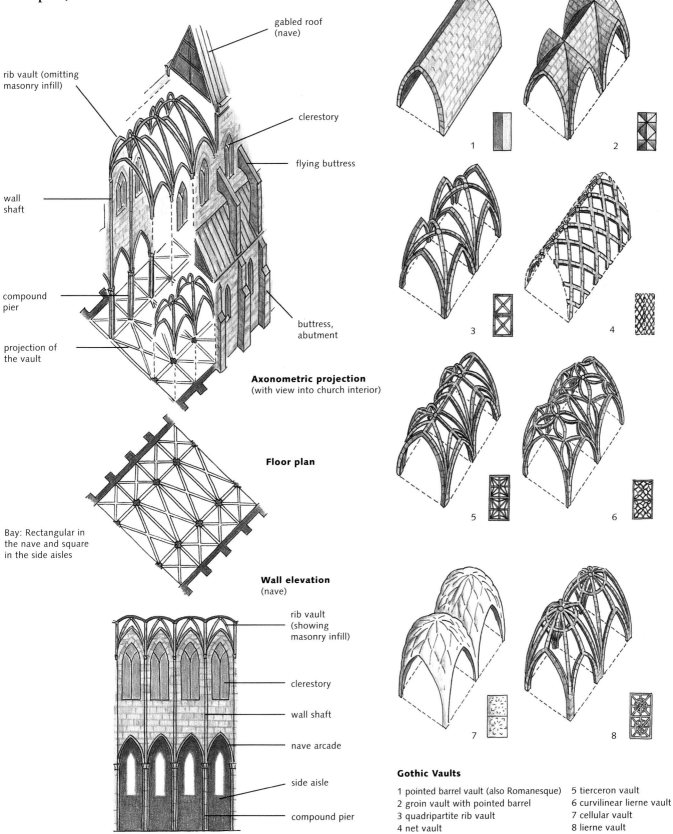

gabled roof
(nave)

rib vault (omitting
masonry infill)

clerestory

flying buttress

wall
shaft

compound
pier

buttress,
abutment

projection of
the vault

Axonometric projection
(with view into church interior)

Floor plan

Bay: Rectangular in
the nave and square
in the side aisles

Wall elevation
(nave)

rib vault
(showing
masonry infill)

clerestory

wall shaft

nave arcade

side aisle

compound pier

Gothic Vaults

1 pointed barrel vault (also Romanesque) 5 tierceron vault
2 groin vault with pointed barrel 6 curvilinear lierne vault
3 quadripartite rib vault 7 cellular vault
4 net vault 8 lierne vault

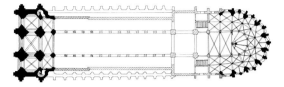

St-Denis, cathedral (former Benedictine abbey church), view into chevet, 1140–1144 (opposite); west end, 1130–1140 (below); exterior of chevet, 1140–1144 and 13th century (right).
The floor plan shows the Carolingian nave and transept with Abbot Suger's early Gothic additions.

St-Denis, Former Benedictine Abbey Church

The Benedictine abbey of St-Denis on the outskirts of Paris played an important role in the history of French royalty. In 754, Charlemagne had himself crowned here as king of the Franks, and Charles II (Charles the Bald) was entombed within its walls.

The relics of St Dionysus, as well as the legend that the church's nave had been dedicated by Christ himself, further contributed to its popularity. In the twelfth century, when the learned and power-conscious Abbot Suger controlled the fate of the monastery, the abbey church became a linchpin of architectural history. Its western addition (1130–1140) and chevet (1140–1144) are considered milestones of Gothic construction.

In neither case, however, can we speak of an entirely new creation. The west porch revives the Carolingian westwork; its massive structure is reminiscent of Norman facades. Nevertheless, the powerful vertical accents created by the buttresses and the sculptural stratification of the entire wall are new. Similarly, the pointed arches in the choir and the vaults on ribs are not an invention of Suger's; builders in Burgundy and Normandy had already been experimenting with these forms for some years. In St-Denis, however, these elements are combined in more consistent patterns, resulting in a new, more open space. The actual wall surface of the double choir gallery is hardly noticeable anymore. The tall windows extend almost to the floor, endowing the room with a majestic light.

Like the transept and the upper sections of the choir, the Carolingian nave was renovated in the high Gothic style during the thirteenth century.

Paris, Cathedral of Notre-Dame, 1163–ca. 1245, choir (above); nave wall (left; the original four-sectioned layout of the nave wall has been reconstructed in front of the crossing); facade of the transept from the southeast (opposite top); west facade (opposite bottom).

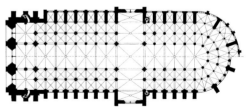

Paris, Notre-Dame

An entire neighborhood on Paris's Île de la Cité was torn down to make room for construction of the Cathedral of Notre-Dame. At 426 feet (130 m) long and 115 ft (35 m) high, this royal cathedral was one of the largest of its day. Pope Alexander III laid the cornerstone in 1163, and by 1245, the ambitious undertaking with its westward-facing facade was largely completed.

Like only a handful of outstanding sacred buildings before it—including St Peter's in Rome and the Abbey Church of Cluny—Notre-Dame was constructed with five aisles, which in this case converge in the double ambulatory of the chevet. It is not only the floor plan that reveals the high demands of the Paris project; builders sought new, spectacular approaches in the vertical construction, as well. The wall of the nave, for instance, appears to be extremely thin, almost fragile. Narrow wall shafts extend uninterrupted by the bandlets commonly used until that time, continuing into the narrow vault ribs, on which rest the gigantic cells of the six-part vault.

Despite its fifty-year building period, the west facade is a paradigm of harmony and clarity that was imitated many times. Its structure is somewhat reminiscent of a triumphal arch, and in fact, the dramatic array of twenty-eight statues in the gallery of kings, as well as the 33-foot (10-m) diameter rose window, display triumphal motifs. The church dispenses with excessively heavy wall reliefs. The three portals, profusely decorated with figures, are dedicated to the Virgin Mary, the Last Judgment, and St Anne.

Laon, Cathedral of Notre-Dame, 1160–1220, overall view with the renovated choir (above); facade, begun ca. 1190 (left); and interior (opposite).

Laon Cathedral rests on a commanding site above the city. Its facade, almost baroque in appearance, is considered one of the high points of Gothic architecture.

Laon, Cathedral

The Cathedral of Notre-Dame in Laon, which was begun around 1160, is considered a jewel among the early Gothic, primarily four-tiered cathedrals. The perfect balance unique to this building stems from the give and take between its flat walls and the profiled "skeleton," which makes the spatial structures especially clear. The builders were evidently quite conscious of this harmony in the church's interior, because when the choir was enlarged in the thirteenth century, its forms were adapted to those of the older sections of the building.

The facade of Laon Cathedral also represents the exceptional, rather than the rule. With the deep hollows of its portals and windows, the towers and tabernacle, it generates a strongly contrasting interplay of light and shadow, material and void, whose perfection is unequaled in any other building of this period. Despite this idiosyncratic, sculptural appearance, however, the facade clearly reflects the three-aisled church interior that lies behind it.

Chartres, Cathedral of Notre-Dame

In 876, Charles the Bald presented the Cathedral of Chartres with an extraordinary relic, the tunic of the Virgin Mary. From that time onward, the small city in the Beauce region was inundated with a nearly endless stream of pilgrims, precipitating constant expansions of the church building. The present cathedral, the embodiment of Gothic architecture, was begun in 1194 following a fire in the previous Romanesque structure, and completed after a short construction period around 1220. Sections of the old building, including the crypt and the west facade, were integrated into the new construction.

Long before visitors arrive at Chartres they can glimpse the majestic cathedral on the hill, with its two mismatched towers

Chartres, cathedral, 1194–
ca. 1220. Left: view from the
south toward the city and the
cathedral reigning over it.

Below: view of the supports
(buttress system) on the
exterior wall.

and its massive system of buttresses. The interior also gives a monumental impression, though at the same time it seems exquisitely delicate and well proportioned, an effect created by the novel, three-tiered elevation (nave arcade, triforium, and clerestory) and the elegant compound drum piers, which are flanked by half or three-quarter columns. Both of these elements became distinctive features of high Gothic architecture. The projecting transept and the spacious double chevet with its chapels could accommodate a large number of the faithful. The gallery of kings on the west facade was built as early as 1145–1155. Its highly expressive jamb figures ushered in a new era in portal design.

Chartres, cathedral, 1194–ca. 1220.
Above left: western rose window, 1210–1220.
Above right: detail of stained glass window depicting stone bearers at work on the construction of a church.
Far right: west portal (Royal Portal), 1145–1155. The tympanum depicts Christ at the Last Judgment; the jamb statues represent the precursors of Christ. These slender figures are seminal Gothic sculptures.
Opposite: interior. The cathedral's stained glass windows bathe the interior in a mystical blue light. Along with the Cathedral of Bourges, the Chartres windows represent the most important ensemble of work in this genre. For the observer, they are as educational as they are enchanting.

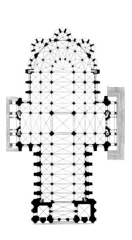

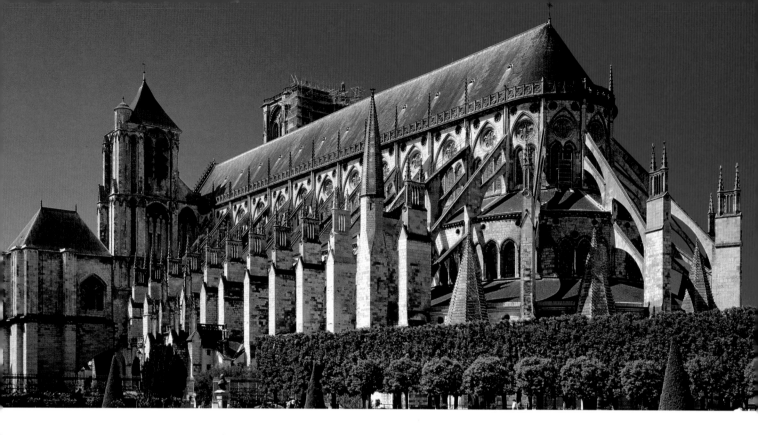

Bourges, Cathedral of St-Étienne

The Cathedral of St-Étienne (St Stephen) in Bourges was begun in 1195 under Archbishop Henri de Sully. Construction took place in two phases. The choir was completed in 1214. After a pause of approximately ten years, work on the nave and the facade was taken up again in 1235 and largely completed by 1255.

The Gothic cathedral at Bourges was thus built during the same period as the cathedrals of Soissons and Chartres; nevertheless, it can scarcely be compared with the latter buildings. The absence of a transept in its floor plan is immediately striking. With five aisles and a double chevet, the church is more closely modeled on Notre-Dame in Paris or the Abbey Church of Cluny.

The differences between Bourges Cathedral and its contemporaries are evident in the exterior, as well. While the Soissons and Chartres churches are characterized by massive abutments and flying buttresses, Bourges astounds the viewer with its almost filigreed structures, which seem to defy the gravitational pull of the earth. Likewise, its interior atmosphere is fundamentally different from that of Soissons and Chartres. The walls appear to be weightless, dissolved into their numerous openings; the wall surfaces appear to be clamped tightly between the gigantic compound piers with their delicate engaged columns. A novel detail of this cathedral is that these columns continue above the capital to meet the ribs of the vault, thus seeming to support it. The entire structure plays with the negation of supports and burdens. Despite these extremely innovative and effective elements, Bourges Cathedral had virtually no imitators, and remained unique in the history of architecture.

The cathedral's treasures include its extraordinary stained glass windows, which offer us insight into the development of this art form between the twelfth and seventeenth centuries.

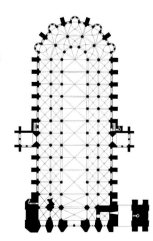

Bourges, Cathedral of St-Étienne, begun 1195, architecture completed ca. 1255, dedicated 1324, renovated in the 14th, 15th, and 16th centuries.
Exterior view from the southeast (opposite top); nave looking east (opposite bottom left); chevet (opposite bottom right); view into the inner side aisle (right).
At 407 ft long, 135 ft wide, and 122 ft (124 x 41 x 37 m) high, Bourges is one of the biggest Gothic cathedrals in France. The relics of St Stephen (St Étienne), which were brought to the city in the 3rd century, are honored within its walls.

Reims, Cathedral of Notre-Dame

From the ninth century onward, French kings were crowned in the Cathedral of Notre-Dame in Reims. For this reason alone, its construction had to satisfy the highest standards. The old church burned down in 1210, and when the cornerstone for the new one was laid the following year, the builders chose as their guideline the most complex nascent construction in existence at the outset of the thirteenth century: Chartres. Many elements of Reims were copied directly from the one begun seventeen years previously, but they were enhanced by local traditions and pre-sented in a new way. A total of five master builders oversaw the project until its completion around 1300. Their names were immortalized in the stone labyrinth built into the cathedral floor. Among the groundbreaking innovations at Reims are the tracery rosettes in the clerestory. Not only did they enhance the allure of the window openings, they also set new technical standards. Their thin mullions could be assembled quickly and could be prefabricated using templates. Tracery work soon became a distinctive element of Gothic architectural decoration.

Opposite: **Reims,** Cathedral of Notre-Dame, begun 1211–ca. 1300, view of the choir from the east. The buttresses are "hollowed out" with tabernacles containing monumental statues of angels.

Below left and right: west facade with figured portals, rose window, and gallery of kings; interior view looking west. As at Chartres Cathedral, compound piers subdivide the three-tiered elevation of the walls.

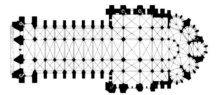

Amiens, Cathedral of Notre-Dame, 1220–1288, main portal (below left) and interior view (below right). The cycle of sculptures around the portals illustrates the History of Salvation; the trumeau (central pier) of the main portal displays the noble image of the resurrected Christ (*Beau Dieu*). It is surrounded by jamb figures of the wise and foolish virgins, the apostles, and the prophets. In the tympanum, an image of the Last Judgment exhorts the faithful to repent.

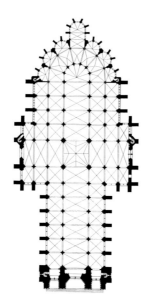

Opposite: The west facade of Amiens Cathedral is more filigree in appearance than any building before it. Three high portals support the gallery and the statue gallery; the rose with flamboyant tracery is flanked by double-tiered towers.

Amiens, Cathedral of Notre-Dame

The Amiens Cathedral was intended to surpass even Chartres and Reims in its splendor. This ambition was only possible because of advances in construction technology that were made at the beginning of the thirteenth century that enabled builders to work faster, less expensively, and more elegantly—that is, even less massively—than ever before. Amiens owes its delicate, light-infused structure to the master builder Robert de Luzarches and his successors, who completed the astonishingly uniform structure between 1220 and 1288. The Cathedral of Amiens marked the beginning of the rayonnant Gothic style in France. Its interior is characterized by a high nave arcade, which extends fully half the height of the three-tiered elevation, as well as a brightly lit triforium in the choir, where the dark end wall is replaced by stained-glass windows.

Even the cathedral's facade—reminiscent of a gossamer web—transports the viewer into another world. Its contrast with the surrounding residential buildings nestled close beside it must have been overwhelming.

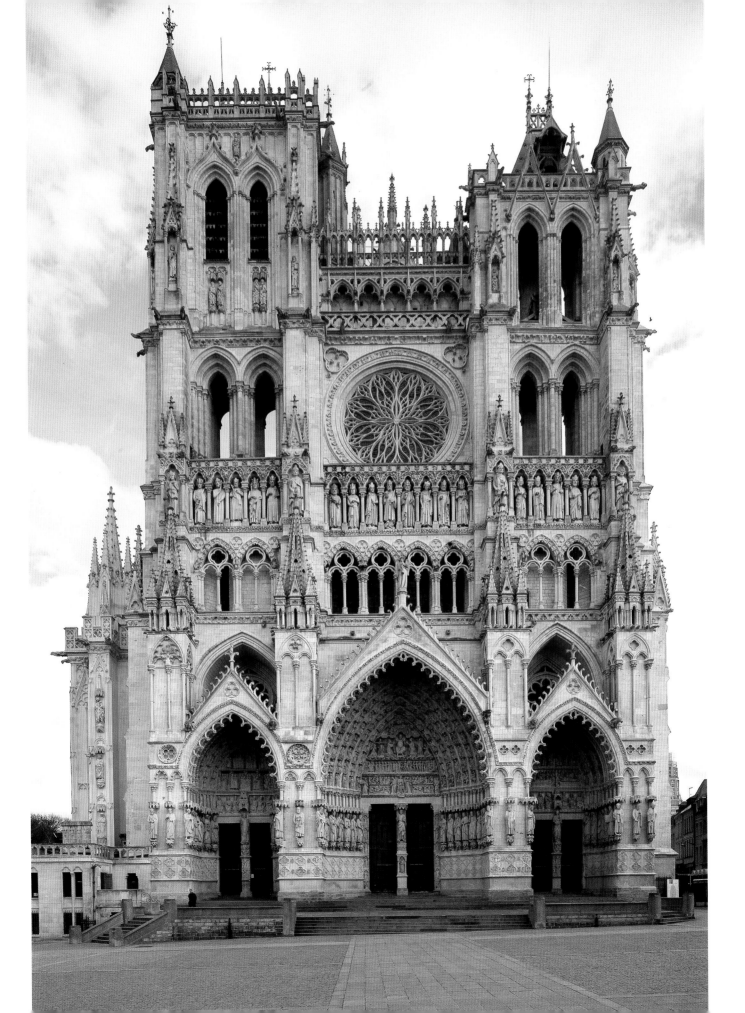

Coutances, Cathedral of Notre-Dame

The Notre-Dame Cathedral in Coutances, in Normandy, represents a special case in the history of architecture. Its Romanesque predecessor did not fall victim to a fire, as in so many other cases; rather, it was rebuilt step by step, from west to east. Coutances therefore allows us to trace not only the gradual advance of technical possibilities, but also the stylistic development of Gothic architecture. Whereas the facade and the nave still contain Romanesque walls, the choir is a completely new construction consisting of high Gothic forms. Its prototypes can be found in the Abbey Church of St-Étienne in Caen as well as the Le Mans Cathedral.

A tall, octagonal crossing tower—a common feature of Norman sacred architecture—looms above the cathedral. In its interior, in particular, this tower displays the highest degree of architectural sophistication.

Coutances, cathedral, rebuilt from 1180, exterior from the east, ca. 1220. The gradation of heights in the chevet is clearly visible: the window-filled walls of the outer and inner ambulatories rise above the radiating chapels.

Auxerre, Cathedral of St-Étienne

The history of the Gothic St-Étienne Cathedral at Auxerre began in 1215, when Bishop Guillaume de Seignelay initiated the new construction of this cathedral dedicated to St Stephen. Since structural problems arose repeatedly in the eastern sections, however, the work continued into the sixteenth century. The old Romanesque crypt had been retained, but this did not seem to be the cause of the many setbacks. Despite the numerous security measures that were added there, it is the choir in particular that is impressive in its elegance and delicacy. The axial chapel opens behind two extremely slender columns. Its vaults have the appearance of fragile canopies draped between the supports.

The exterior of the building reflects its ever-changing history. The facade already typifies the late Gothic flamboyant style; the church's southern tower was never completed.

Auxerre, Cathedral of St-Étienne, 1215 to 16th century. Above: exterior view. Left: view into the axial chapel of the chevet, completed 1234.

Royal Chapels

In ages in which emperors and kings invoked the Divine Right, the court or palace chapel held an extraordinary status within the royal residence. It is therefore not surprising that artistic means were employed to underscore their national-political significance. From the time of Louis IX (also called Saint Louis, 1223–1270), not one but two buildings have been preserved in the Paris region that outshine many others in sumptuousness if not in size. These are the Ste-Chapelle at the palace of St-Germain-en-Laye and the Ste-Chapelle on the Île de la Cité, once part of the Cité palace. Both are thought to have been built by Pierre de Montreuil, the builder of the southern transept facade of Notre Dame, but no definitive evidence has been preserved in this regard. Nevertheless, the quality of their construction and the sophistication of their furnishings speak a language of their own. In St-Germain-en-Laye, it is the multilayered complexity of the walls that is presented with such relish and artistry. Unfortunately, the original colored panes of glass, which provided still further painterly effects, did not survive.

In the upper chapel of the Ste-Chapelle in Paris, the stained glass has been preserved and is largely responsible for the unique atmosphere of the space. Here, the walls have been completely dissolved into stained glass panels and frames—a glass shrine that provided a sacred setting for the king and his cult. The Ste-Chapelle contains the relic of Christ's crown of thorns, the worship of which was connected to that of the French

Above left and right: **St-Germain-en-Laye** (Yvelines near Paris), La Ste-Chapelle, begun 1238, interior and exterior views. The palatine chapel of Saint Louis experimented with the dissolution of wall surfaces.

Below and opposite: **Paris,** La Ste-Chapelle, chapel of the former Palais de la Cité, begun 1241, dedicated 1248, view into the lower chapel (below) and the upper chapel with its exquisite stained glass windows (opposite).

Above: **Toulouse,** Church of the Jacobins, ca. 1285–1385. The double-aisled building with its artful vaulting is a masterpiece of southern French monastic architecture. The width of the space and the windows that encircle the entire room foreshadow the late Gothic style.

Opposite top: **Albi,** Cathedral of Ste-Cécile, 1282–ca. 1330. Albi Cathedral has a fortress-like appearance and is somewhat reminiscent of the cathedrals of northern France. The interior space, however, supported by piers and transverse barrel vaults, is very much in the tradition of southern France and Catalonia.

Opposite bottom: **Narbonne,** Cathedral of St-Just, 1272–1354, view of the high Gothic chevet. The construction of the nave was repeatedly postponed, since it would have called for the demolition of part of the city walls. The project was finally abandoned altogether in the eighteenth century.

Gothic Architecture in Southern France

In the second half of the thirteenth century, the impulses of Gothic cathedral architecture, which had originated in northern France, began to spread throughout large areas of Europe. In southern France, however, these new styles and techniques were not necessarily embraced with open arms. On the one hand, the Midi region had already developed its own rich architectural tradition; on the other, the Gothic style of the Île de France was intimately associated with the crown, and could be interpreted as a distasteful "royalist" demonstration of power.

To put this in context: the twelfth and thirteenth centuries had been a period of crises and unrest in the Languedoc region. Attempts at independence on the part of the counts of Toulouse, the Cathar uprisings and charges of heresy that resulted in the murder and pillaging of the Albigensian Crusades, and finally, the bloody conquest by King Louis VIII, who aimed to extend his kingdom as far as the Mediterranean and forced Count Raymond VII of Toulouse to capitulate in 1229—all of these events contributed to the fact that there was distrust if not downright enmity between the northern and southern regions of France.

Nonetheless, in the last third of the thirteenth century, many attributes of northern French cathedrals were adopted in the south: the basilica structure, vertical progression, elaborate architectural ornamentation. Whether this development can be seen as the result of cooperation between the clergy and the crown or simply as an expression of desire for innovation is an open question. In any case, the cathedrals built at Narbonne, Toulouse, and Rodez satisfied the highest standards of aesthetics and perfection. Their master builders made use of the newest technologies that led to the streamlining of the building trade.

Ste-Cécile Cathedral in Albi (begun in 1282) is the most impressive example of the endurance of regional mannerisms in the Gothic architecture of the Midi. The church looks more like a fortress than a house of worship: compact brick walls with shaft-like windows surround the central space. Only the beveled buttresses break its austere lines and create dark chapels, which once extended through the entire height of the space. The density and darkness of the church's atmosphere was originally perhaps even more pronounced, as the galleries and lower windows were not added until the late fifteenth century.

The Church of the Jacobins in Toulouse (begun ca. 1285) was the mother church of the Dominican Order, which largely oversaw the Papal Inquisition. This, too, is a hall church, here divided into two aisles, one for friars and the other for laity. The highlight of its singular architecture is the *Palmier*, or palm tree—a column at the eastern end of the church from which the ribs branch out into a star-shaped apse vault.

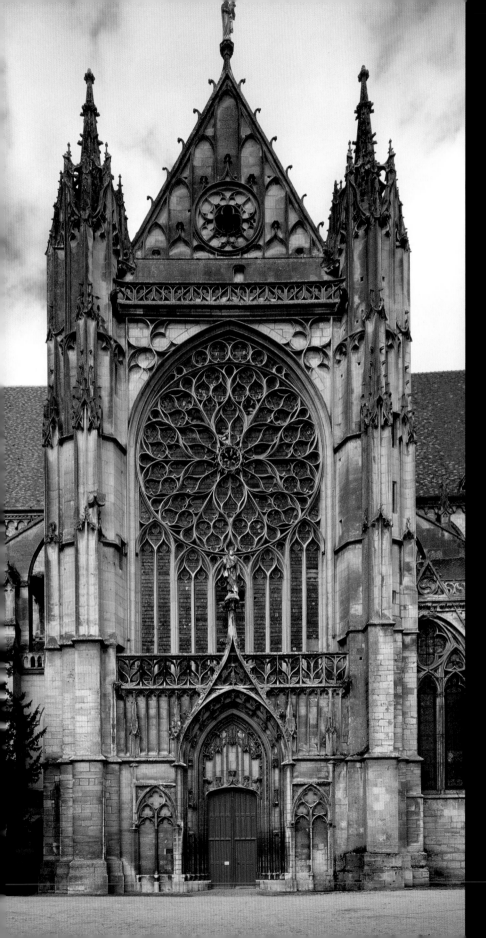

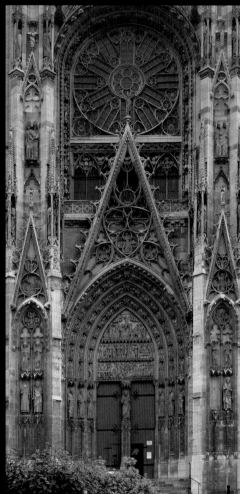

Above: **Rouen,** St-Ouen, crossing tower, ca. 1440–1515. The massive crossing tower of the former Norman abbey church was constructed in two phases. Its quadrangular lower tiers were built ca. 1440; the crowning octagonal section near the end of the 15th century.

Left: **Sens,** St-Étienne Cathedral, south transept facade, 1490–1512. Martin Chambiges designed the flamboyant facade, which was added to the Gothic building from 1130.

Opposite: **Bourg-en-Bresse,** Brou Abbey Church, 1513–1532, rood screen.
Brou was founded in 1506 by the Dutch regent Margaret of Austria, intended as the burial site for her deceased husband, Philip the Fair of Savoy. With its exquisite architecture and splendid decoration, the church, designed by Loys van Boghem, is a jewel of late Gothic architecture.

The architecture of the late Gothic period was long considered to be an art of decline that made no further creative contributions to the high Gothic building arts of the thirteenth century. And in fact, between the fourteenth and sixteenth centuries, until the Renaissance arrived in France with Francis I, the "classic cathedral" remained the model that was copied in countless variations. Nevertheless, magnificent works of art were created—buildings that could withstand any comparison with their predecessors. Their ornamentation and tracery forms transmuted and evolved until they took on a masterful life of their own, with an ingenuity that never ceases to amaze. The French term *flamboyant*—that is, flickering like a flame—perfectly captures the dynamics of these elements. Walls and facades were decked out in "lace gowns" that swirled decoratively around the structures.

The art of stonecutting achieved a level of precision and subtlety that approached that of goldsmithery. Yet the late Gothic is not a purely decorative style. In the fifteenth and sixteenth centuries, in particular, enormous spaces were created that clearly illustrate the well-planned harmonization and fusion of structural elements. Light, which now flowed into the building interiors through huge, bright windows, made its own contribution to the new "dematerialized" sense of space.

In France, the late Gothic period began around 1380, but it only came to full fruition after the Hundred Years' War ended in 1453. Many churches whose construction had been interrupted by the confusion of war were subsequently completed in the late Gothic style. At the same time, however, many completely new and prestigious urban buildings were also built in this period.

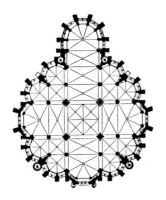

Opposite: **Trier,** former Dom-stiftskirche Unserer Lieben Frau (Collegiate Church of Our Dear Lady), begun before 1235 (?), view from the east. The eastern arm of this cruciform, central-plan church has been extended to house the choir.

Trier, Liebfrauenkirche

The Liebfrauenkirche (Church of Our Dear Lady) in Trier, along with St Elisabeth in Marburg, is considered one of the earliest examples of pure Gothic architecture in Germany. The structure, which was begun before 1235, did indeed adopt French motifs, particularly from the area around Reims, such as compound piers, two-tiered construction, tracery windows, and ribbed vaulting. However, they are combined here in an innovative style.

In contrast to its predecessors, the Liebfrauenkirche is a central-plan building consisting of two short, three-aisled cross arms with apsidioles set in their corners. The eastern arm, containing the choir, is somewhat longer. The layout—an unusual one for a parish church—may be based on an earlier, late antique building, which would also explain the peculiar rearrangement of French structural elements.

Marburg, Church of St Elisabeth

The Hospital and Pilgrimage Church of St Elisabeth in Marburg, on the Lahn River, is a close stylistic cousin of the Liebfrauen-kirche in Trier. Here, too, builders copied early Gothic architectural forms from the Champagne region and elaborated upon them further.

St Elisabeth was begun in 1235, over the grave of Elizabeth of Hungary (also called Elizabeth of Thuringia), who had died four years earlier and was immediately canonized. Elizabeth was a princess who enjoyed enormous popularity due to her many charitable activities. The church, built at the behest of the Order of Teutonic Knights, combines two contrasting spatial forms, the hall of the nave and the triconch of the choir, the latter being a typical element of the Rhineland Romanesque style. Ever since the fourteenth century, Hessian landgraves have been entombed here, always seeking to be placed as close to the saint as possible.

Above and right: **Marburg an der Lahn,** Hospital and Pilgrimage Church of St Elisabeth, begun 1235, interior of the nave facing west and exterior view from the southeast showing the triconch choir.

Strasbourg, minster, 1250–1275. Interior view of the nave facing west (above) and exterior view of the nave and late Romanesque transept (right).

Strasbourg, Minster

Work on the new Gothic nave of Strasbourg Minster began in approximately 1250, although the choir and transept had been completed in the late Romanesque style just shortly before. This structure, which was completed in 1275, was among the most modern buildings that had been erected in France or within the Holy Roman Empire at that time. Its prototype was evidently St-Denis near Paris, since both churches contain piers with engaged columns that extend unbroken to the spring of the vault, a glazed triforium, and windows decorated with tracery work.

The harmonization of these elements with the older transept posed a particular artistic challenge. After the completion of the nave, the cornerstone was laid for the magnificent west facade (illus. p. 2), whose design is attributed to Erwin von Steinbach. Although the truth of this legend seems doubtful today, Goethe nevertheless composed a romantic memorial to him.

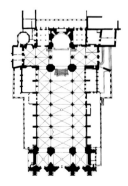

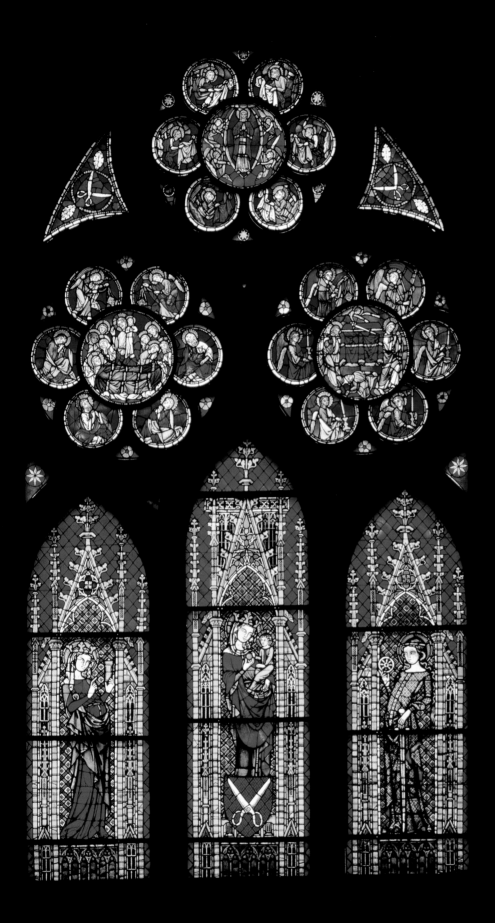

Freiburg, Cathedral

Like most of the sacred buildings of the Middle Ages, Freiburg Cathedral was not completed in a single continuous process, and was therefore not built in a "pure," consistent style. In fact, the juxtapositions of styles seem to have been experienced, if not quite as the norm, then as an invigorating challenge. This is particularly true in the case of the Dom Unserer Lieben Frau (Cathedral of Our Dear Lady), which was begun around 1200 at the behest of Duke Berthold of Zähringen. As was often the case, construction of the late Romanesque eastern sections preceded that of the nave, which was reworked in the early Gothic style.

In 1354, Master Johannes von Gmünd, a member of the Parler family, began new construction of the polygonal choir, including an ambulatory and axial chapels. The reticulated vaults that cover the raised choir, however, were only completed in 1510.

The church's soaring western tower with its openwork tracery spire became a milestone in the history of architecture, "the most beautiful tower in Christendom." In the absence of any prominent antetype, its audacious construction and refined stylistic character can scarcely be explained. The most immediate models can be found in the west facade of Strasbourg and in "Plan F" for the Cologne Cathedral. The similarity of these buildings' motifs confirms that by this time, architectural drawing had become an indispensable prerequisite for the transfer of forms.

Freiburg, cathedral, begun ca. 1200.

Left: Late Gothic window in the nave; the lower sections display the attributes of the guilds that donated the panes of glass, in this case, the tailors' window.

Opposite top left: View into the tracery spire of the tower, after 1301.

Opposite bottom left: Interior of the choir.

Opposite far right: View of the cathedral from the southeast.

Cologne, Cathedral

For the German Romantics, Cologne Cathedral represented the epitome of German medieval architecture. From an architectural-historical point of view, however, it is more French than any French cathedral could ever have been.

The present cathedral stands on the same site as numerous predecessors. Its construction was planned as early as 1164, when the relics of the Three Kings came into the possession of the archbishop of Cologne, but the cornerstone was only laid in 1248, by Archbishop Konrad von Hochstaden. The choir was built under the direction of several well-known master builders and dedicated in 1322, but the cathedral was far from complete at that time. Work continued into the nineteenth century, when the transept facade, nave clerestory, and most of the west facade were finally completed.

Nevertheless—or perhaps for this very reason—Cologne Cathedral appears to be a "perfect" example of the French Gothic style. No experiments were carried out here; rather, builders drew from a checklist of many previously tested solutions. The templates for Cologne's ideal structure can be found in the cathedrals at Amiens and Reims, in the Abbey Church of St-Denis, and even in the clerestory of the never-completed but nonetheless spectacular Beauvais Cathedral.

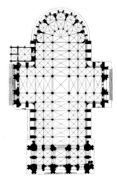

Cologne, cathedral, cornerstone laid 1248; construction ceased 1560; completed in the 19th century.

Left: Exterior of the choir, dedicated in 1322.

Opposite: View into the interior and choir, which is surrounded by an ambulatory and seven axial chapels.

Naumburg, Cathedral of St Peter and St Paul

The statues in Naumburg Cathedral are masterpieces of European Gothic sculpture. In contrast to France, where figures and decor tended to be secondary to architecture, the twelve life-sized founder figures in the west choir seem to share equal status with the early Gothic architecture. Like the church's famous western rood screen, they are the work of the legendary Naumburg Master, a sculptor who was educated in France and maintained a flourishing workshop. Executed around 1250, they depict ancestors of the houses of Ekkehard and Wettin with tremendous freedom; the figures are portrayed in contemporary clothing and as animated individuals, something no earlier artist had dared to do in a similar context. The Christ figure in the western rood screen, which opens into the narthex of the west choir like a church portal, also displays an unusual degree of realism. All these figures were rendered in color, making their appearance all the more striking.

Naumburg, Cathedral of St Peter and St Paul, begun before 1213 on the site of an earlier building. Completed in the 14th century after numerous changes in plan. Above: View of the east choir, expanded in 1330, and the cloister.

Below: Interior view of the west choir, begun ca. 1250, with the founder figures sculpted by the Naumburg Master and his workshop. Their intercession was thought to assist the living in entering Paradise.

Opposite: Portal of the western rood screen, ca. 1250, by the Naumburg Master. The central pier depicts the dying Christ between Mary and John. His countenance is streaked with blood, his gaze defeated.

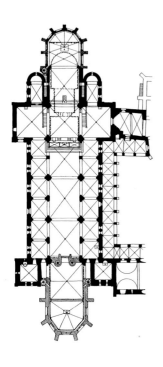

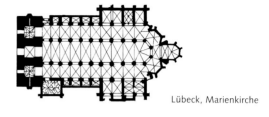

Lübeck, Marienkirche

Left: **Lübeck,** Marienkirche (Parish Church of St Mary), ca. 1266–1351, view of the choir, whose design was modeled after French prototypes.

Below: **Prenzlau,** Marienkirche (Church of St Mary), after 1325. The facade is crowned by a richly decorated, triangular gable.

Opposite: **Chorin,** former Cistercian abbey church, 1273–1334. The facade is documented as the work of Master Conrad.

The Marienkirche in Lübeck and the Northern German Brick Gothic Style

In the regions of northern and eastern Europe where there was little natural stone, builders began constructing prestigious structures of brick as early as the twelfth century. Their techniques originated in Lombardy; thus, the first brick Romanesque churches were also modeled after northern Italian prototypes. As the Gothic architecture of northern France became more widespread, the Baltic and Hanseatic regions also began to adopt new building guidelines. The Marienkirche (Church of St Mary) in Lübeck, which was redesigned in the second half of the thirteenth century and modeled directly on French cathedrals, became paradigmatic for this movement. Its new basilica plan (the recently completed hall of the nave had been modified accordingly) and choir, which has chapel vaults that merge with those of the ambulatory bays, set the standards for countless other parish churches and cathedrals in northern Germany, Scandinavia, and Poland.

The adaptation of Gothic decorative forms to the new building material presented a particular challenge. Whereas capitals, tracery and friezes can be sculpted in stone relatively smoothly, there were clear limits to what was possible when working with brittle bricks. Yet the builders made a virtue of necessity: the facades of the brick churches are characterized by an obviously construction-based decorative style. In many cases, the contrasting placement of glazed bricks provides the walls with lively, colorful accents.

Principles of Construction

Above: **Salem,** former Cistercian abbey church, dedicated 1414. In the 15th century, even the Cistercian orders, which were generally opposed to decoration, allowed themselves the luxury of tracery windows.

Opposite: **Regensburg,** cathedral, begun after 1273, detail of the nave with buttresses and flying buttresses.

The master builders and architects of the Middle Ages sought to transport worshippers who entered their spaces into otherworldly spheres. They achieved this through the use of mathematical principles and geometric figures, which they saw as the expression of cosmic harmony.

The complicated buttress systems of Gothic cathedrals, the ever more complex tracery windows, whose designs were based on the spokes of a compass, and finally, the impressive floor plans—all these would be unimaginable without the necessary intellectual basis. A highly developed system of logistics allowed for the execution of these "intellectual constructs." Gothic builders' yards were organized and networked at a level approaching contemporary standards—vitally important conditions for the technical realization of their projects.

Ulm, Minster

A magnificent tower soaring 530 feet (161 m) into the air dominates Ulm Minster, the parish church of this city on the Danube. Its bold construction rivals the contemporary cathedrals in appearance; this is no accident, as the project was commissioned in 1392 to Ulrich von Ensingen, a highly gifted master builder who was the master mason at Strasbourg and Esslingen at the time.

Schwäbisch-Gmünd

Heiligkreuzkirche (Church of the Holy Cross) in Schwäbisch-Gmünd is among the most innovative architectural monuments of the late Gothic period in Germany. The work of the Parler family of master builders, it is one of the earliest hall churches in Swabia. The spatial separation of the choir is another new feature; its design is attributed to Heinrich, father of the famous Peter Parler.

Left and below: **Ulm,** minster, exterior and interior views, choir 1377–1383, nave by 1405, design of the west tower 1392–1399.

Opposite: **Schwäbisch-Gmünd,** Church of the Holy Cross, interior; nave 1310–1315, choir 1351–1380, dedicated 1410, vault 1491–1521.

Bavarian Hall Churches

Hall churches, in which the central and side aisles are equal in height and united under a single roof, took on a special significance in the late Gothic period. Many urban parish churches, particularly in Bavaria and Saxony, adopted this architectural style; nevertheless, it is no longer tenable to speak of the hall church as a bourgeois building form. Two of the most beautiful examples of this genre can be found at residences of the Royal House of Wittelsbach, in Landshut and in Munich. St Martin in Landshut served simultaneously as the palace church and the parish church.

The Church of St Martin in Landshut is the *magnum opus* of Hans von Burghausen, who is considered the founder of the Bavarian school of building in the fifteenth century. Visitors are struck by the stunningly wide space. Narrow octagonal piers support the 95-foot (29-m) high decorative lierne vault; with a diameter of only 39 inches (1 m), they seem more like slender poles than load-bearing supports. Glittering light streams into the whitewashed brick interior through its high Gothic windows. A monument to the skilled master builder can be found on the outer wall of the church.

The Frauenkirche (Cathedral of Our Lady) in Munich, whose cornerstone was laid in 1468, completes the cycle of great Gothic hall churches. Its characteristic onion domes (actually ogees) still characterize the city's silhouette today. Although the Frauenkirche is a typological relative of St Martin in Landshut, its interior atmosphere seems much cooler; its piers are more massive and are placed more closely together.

Above: **Landshut,** St Martin, begun ca. 1380 by Hans von Burghausen, continued after 1432 by Hans von Stethaimer and others, view into the interior.

Opposite and left: **Munich,** Frauenkirche, 1468–1494, apogees 1525, interior and exterior views. The architect of the new building, founded by Duke Sigismund, was Jörg von Halsbach; its primarily baroque furnishings were replaced by a neogothic decor in the nineteenth century.

Vienna, Stephansdom

The walls of the Stephansdom (Cathedral of St Stephen), one of Vienna's most recognizable landmarks, have borne witness to a turbulent history. Constant renovations and reconstructions, interventions by its patrons, and repeated fires shaped the appearance of the cathedral, which evolved from Romanesque to Renaissance style. Among the oldest parts are the essentially Romanesque western section with its Giant's Door. The current cathedral was dedicated in 1263. Work on the three-aisled hall choir began in 1304; it is known as the "Albertine Choir" after its patrons, Albrecht I and Albrecht II. After its completion, the remaining parts of the church were redesigned, including the towers. The architectural ornamentation and sculpture, including the exquisite pulpit designed by Anton Pilgram, mark the transition from the late Gothic into the Renaissance.

Vienna, Stephansdom, 13th–15th centuries. Above: stained glass window depicting an angel swinging a thurible, ca.1340; right: west facade with Giant's Door, 1230/40–1263, reintegrating older sculptures; opposite: pulpit designed by Anton Pilgram, 1514–1515. Half-length portraits of the church fathers appear around the outside of the pulpit; at the bottom right of the photograph is a man looking out of a window (the "window man"), thought to be Pilgram's self-portrait.

Above and right: **Basel,** minster, rebuilt ca. 1160–ca. 1500, pulpit, Hans von Nußdorf, 1486, and Georgsturm (St George's Tower), Ulrich von Ensingen, 1421–1429.

Switzerland

With the cathedrals at Lausanne and Geneva, Switzerland lays claim to two of the earliest Gothic cathedrals outside France. Both churches were begun in the second half of the twelfth century and contain typical features of the Burgundian early Gothic style: triforia, three-tiered wall elevations, and sculptural decoration on the piers. However, not all of Switzerland's sacred buildings were modeled after French prototypes. The Basel Minster, which was rebuilt between 1185 and 1229 after a devastating fire, features galleries that strongly recall those of Modena Cathedral. The northern portal (St Gallus' Door), with its intricate program of sculptures, dates from the Romanesque period. In the fifteenth century, two towers were added to the west facade of the sandstone building; the Georgsturm on the north

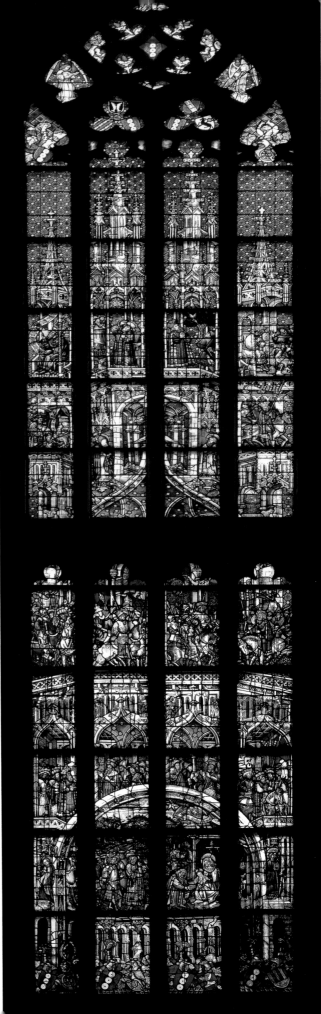

Above and right: **Bern,** minster,
begun 1421, completed with tower
1894. Above: view from the south;
right: the window of the Three Kings
in the choir, ca. 1453.

side was built according to a design by Ulm master builder
Ulrich von Ensingen and elicited admiration all over Europe.

In addition to Basel Minster, magnificent examples of late
Gothic architecture survive in many locations in Switzerland.
They bear witness to the increasing prosperity of the parishes in
the fourteenth and fifteenth centuries. St Vincenz in Bern rises
high above the city on the Aar River. Its first master mason,
beginning in 1421, was Matthäus Ensinger, the son of Ulrich.
Unfortunately, unlike his father, he did not get to complete a
spectacular work: the 330-foot- (100-m-) high tower could not
be completed until the nineteenth century. The famous window
of the Three Kings in the choir dates from the mid-fifteenth
century. Donated by the von Ringoltingen family, it depicts the
legend of the biblical Magi in unusual detail.

Prague, Cathedral of St Vitus

Prague, one of the wealthiest cities in the Holy Roman Empire, became an archbishopric in 1344. Construction of the Cathedral of St Vitus on the grounds of Prague Castle began immediately, and Matthias von Arras was commissioned as master mason. Before his death in 1352, he managed to complete the choir gallery and main choir arcade in the southern French Gothic style, thereby laying the foundations for this monumental structure. Arras was succeeded by Peter Parler, who had previously worked on the Church of the Holy Cross in Schwäbisch-Gmünd. Parler introduced significant technical innovations that subtly increased the dynamics of the interior. For example, he dispensed with the transverse arches separating the bays in the nave, thereby creating a new kind of visually continuous type of vault from west to east that spans the bays with decorative, interlacing diagonal ribs. Parler's second ground-breaking innovation was in the triforium, whose window-filled back wall joined with the panes in the clerestory to create a single, light-flooded membrane of glass. The subtly advancing and receding wall surfaces of the triforium create a unique, wavelike, rhythmic

effect on the upper walls of the nave. In breaking away from traditional methods, Peter Parler brought a playful lightness and originality to sacred architecture. The famous triforium busts in Prague Cathedral are a testament to Parler's awareness of this fact: along with the family of Emperor Charles IV and the archbishops of Prague, the two master builders of the cathedral are also portrayed.

Prague Cathedral contains yet another masterpiece by the great sculptor and architect: the tomb of King Přemysl Otakar I, built in 1377. It is the only work of Parler's here that has been documented and dated in written sources.

Prague, Cathedral of St Vitus, begun after 1344 by Matthias von Arras, continued by Peter Parler and his sons Wenzel and Johan after 1352; construction ceased in the 15th century.
Exterior view of the choir (opposite); view of the interior facing east (left); detail of a wall segment with triforium busts (above).

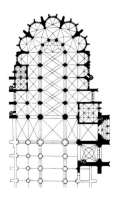

Late Gothic in the Netherlands

The historical Netherlands—parts of which are now northern France, Belgium, and Holland—experienced an economic and cultural flowering during the late Middle Ages. In the flourishing trade towns, wealthy citizens held sway over the communities and built stone monuments to themselves in the form of town halls, churches, and assembly halls. For the most part, the sacred architecture of the Netherlands copied the styles of the neighboring regions of France; depending upon the geological setting, builders used either dressed stone or brick. A monumental quality and a penchant for lavish, late-Gothic ornamentation are common characteristics of all of these buildings.

In the mid-fourteenth century, two imposing buildings were erected in Brabant that ushered in what was known as the Brabant Gothic style: the Mechelen Abbey Church (now a cathedral) and Onze-Lieve-Vrouwekathedraal (Cathedral of Our Lady) in Antwerp. In both churches, builders adopted the structure of France's high Gothic cathedrals, but overlaid them with a network of decorative patterns. Tracery, latticework, lancets, and quatrefoils are superimposed on the wall surfaces, giving them the appearance of a delicate cocoon. The origin of this decorative style can be found on the other side of the English Channel. English builders began using similar illusionary techniques to decorate their cathedrals as early as the first decades of the thirteenth century.

The Nieuwe Kerk (New Church) in Delft, which was begun in 1384 (with the addition of the choir after 1453), demonstrates how far-reaching and enduring the Brabant decorative style was. Here, the clerestory wall is hollowed out with niches that at one time were encased in delicate tracery lattices. The interior atmosphere in the Delft church, however, is completely

Above and right: **Antwerp,** Onze-Lieve-Vrouwekathedraal (Cathedral of Our Lady), begun 1352, interior and exterior views. With its five aisles, to which chapels were added in the 15th century, it is the largest sacred building in what was then the Netherlands. The (unfinished) tower front was begun by Peter Appelman and continued by Herman de Waghemakere and his sons.

Opposite left: **Utrecht,** Cathedral of St Martin, 1254–1517. The 367-foot (112-m)-high tower, built by Master Jan of Hainaut, was added to the nave between 1321 and 1383.

Opposite right: **Delft,** Nieuwe Kerk (New Church), begun 1384, choir after 1453, interior view. With its massive drum piers, the Nieuwe Kerk in Delft was modeled after the abbey church in Mechelen.

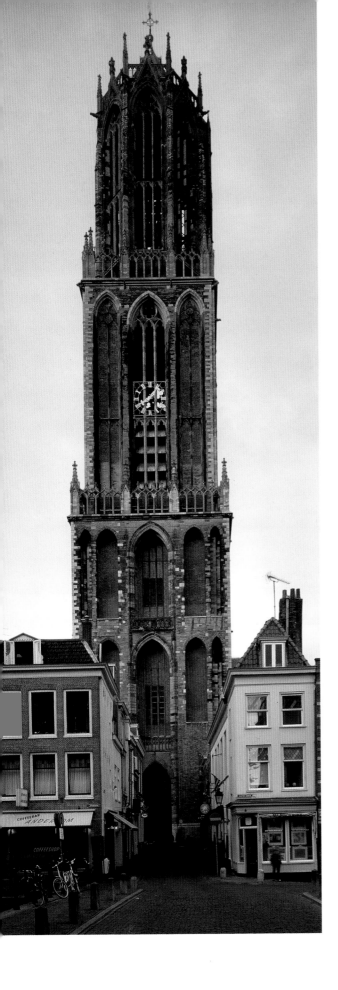

different. Instead of the five-aisled hall-like space of Antwerp Cathedral, here we find a compact, box-like room enclosed by a wooden roof.

Church towers served a double function in the Netherlands. In addition to their religious purpose, they were used for community functions and served as a symbol of bourgeois power that could be seen from far and wide. The building of towers and spires became a source of pride in the towns of the Netherlands; each community tried to build a higher and more complex monument. The tower of the Cathedral of St Martin in Utrecht, with its artful, openwork octagonal spire designed by Master Jan of Hainaut, became the prototype for many later structures.

Gothic in Scandinavia

Various developmental threads converged in the Gothic sacred architecture of Scandinavia. As everywhere else in Europe, the structure of the church space was dominated by French standards. Nevertheless, English principles of decoration also made themselves felt here, and in the brick structures especially, the influence of Lübeck artists is evident.

The Odense Domkirke (Cathedral of St Canute) in Denmark was rebuilt at the end of the fourteenth century after numerous fires. Its interior is striking for its elegant, lavishly molded arcades. The Gothic cathedral in Uppsala, Sweden, was subjected to a renovation in the neogothic style in the nineteenth century; it then underwent a radical "reverse restoration" in the 1970s. The church of the Løgum Abbey (*Locus Dei*/Place of God) is a prime example of Cistercian architecture. Following the removal of layers of white lime, the attractively contrasting colors of the glazed bricks are once again clearly visible. A typical feature of Denmark's Gothic church architecture is the crow-stepped gable, subdivided by blind niches, a motif borrowed from secular architecture.

Left: **Odense,** Domkirke (Cathedral of St Canute), begun 11th century, Gothic structure late 14th century, view into the nave.

Opposite top: **Uppsala,** cathedral, interior and exterior views, 1287–1485, renovated in neogothic style by Helgo Zettervall 1885–1893, reverse restoration after 1970.

Opposite below: **Løgum Abbey,** founded 1173, church and cloister 1225–1325, view from the northeast.

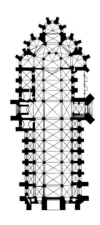

Uppsala Cathedral

Gdansk (Danzig), St Mary

St Mary in Danzig is one of the largest churches of the Middle Ages, and one of the most imposing brick buildings ever built. The three-aisle hall church with chapels, a high transept, and square end choir, was erected from 1343 to 1502. The nave, which measures 346 x 217 feet (105 x 66 m), can hold over 25,000 worshippers, and its 256-foot (78-m) tall tower dominates the skyline of this ancient Hanseatic city. The church's famous net vaults, masterful examples of late Gothic architecture, were built between 1498 and 1502 under the direction of city architectural master Heinrich Hetzel. Similar vaults can be found in the Albrechtsburg in Meissen. St Mary in Danzig was badly damaged during World War II, when more than forty percent of the vaulting collapsed. Its reconstruction is as great a technical achievement as the original.

Right: **Gdansk (Danzig),** St Mary 1343–1502. Interior with net vaults by Heinrich Hetzel, 1498–1502.

Stargard Szczeciński, Church of the Blessed Virgin

This monumental brick church in Stargard Szczeciński is one of the most significant Gothic buildings in Poland. Centrally located inside the city walls, it was begun in 1292 as a hall church. In the fifteenth century it was transformed into a basilica with the addition of chapels and galleries. Hinrich Brunsberg, one of the greatest architects of the Baltic Sea region, built the chevet dating from approximately 1400. One of the most unusual features is the triforium between the ambulatory and clerestory, a rare feature in brick buildings. The nave of the church was modified during early-sixteenth-century renovations. The star vaulting stems from this period, although it had to be completely rebuilt following a fire in 1635.

Left and opposite: **Stargard Szczeciński,** nave of the Church of the Blessed Virgin, 1282, renovated during the 14th through 17th centuries, with chevet by Hinrich Brunsberg (opposite) ca 1400

Early English Gothic and the Cathedrals at Canterbury, Lincoln, and Wells

Early English is the first of the three phases of Gothic architecture in the British Isles. It was popular roughly from 1170 to 1240 and, with some exceptions, is similar to early Gothic in France, from which it is derived. As was true elsewhere in Europe, the agents of transmission were the Cistercians. The architectural forms favored by the austere, strictly regulated monastic order first influenced buildings and stylistic developments in France, and later in other parts of the Roman Catholic world. Traveling clerics and architects also spread their ideas. This is certainly the case with Canterbury Cathedral (which houses the grave of the martyred St Thomas Becket, who was murdered there). After it burned in 1174, the resident monks organized a competition for the design of its replacement. The winner was William of Sens, a Frenchman. Despite the requirement that the new cathedral be raised on the foundations of the old walls, William's design was an innovative work, very much in the French style. The monk's choir was elegantly subdivided into three sections. Details in black Purbeck marble enhance the vertical elements, and six-part rib vaults cover the interior space. Canterbury Cathedral's double transept, a feature that would become

Above: **Lincoln,** cathedral, 1220–1240, interior.

Right: **Canterbury,** cathedral, 1175–1184, exterior from the southeast.

Lincoln

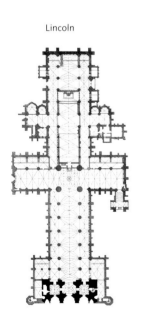

Canterbury

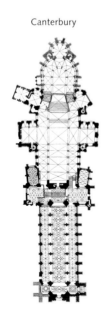

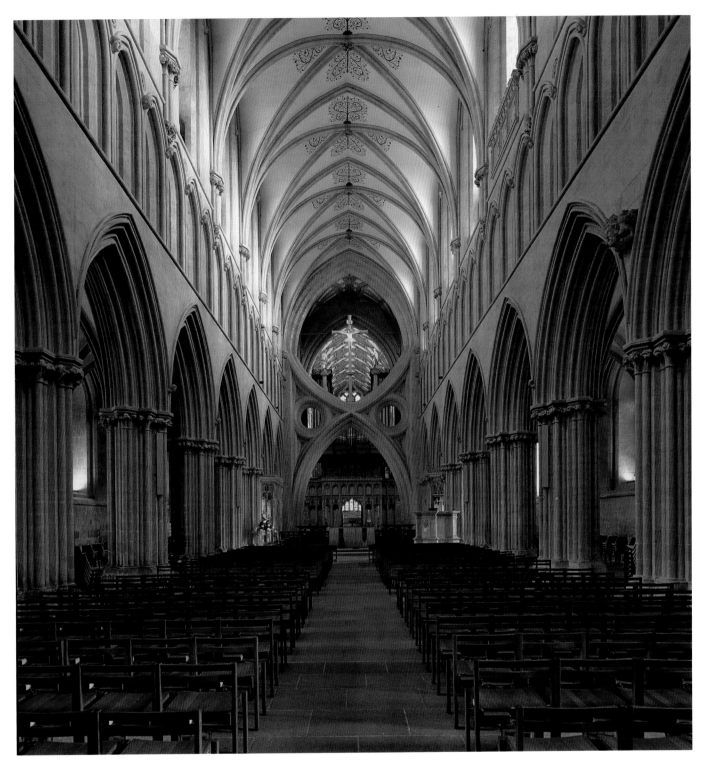

characteristic of English sacred architecture, appears here for the first time. After William fell from a scaffold in 1178, his successor, William the Englishman, continued his work, including the Gothic Trinity Chapel.

Lincoln Cathedral surpasses its predecessor Canterbury, at least where fantasy is concerned. The main choir vault by Gottfried Noiers is known as the "crazy vault." In western England, Wells Cathedral took French architectural forms and translated them in still another way. The nave arcade and triforium in Wells are extremely fine, almost graphically delineated. When the cathedral's crossing threatened to collapse in 1338, master mason William Joy braced it with bold, intersecting pointed arches.

Wells, Cathedral, 1180–1240, view of the nave braced with "scissor arches" by William Joy in 1338.

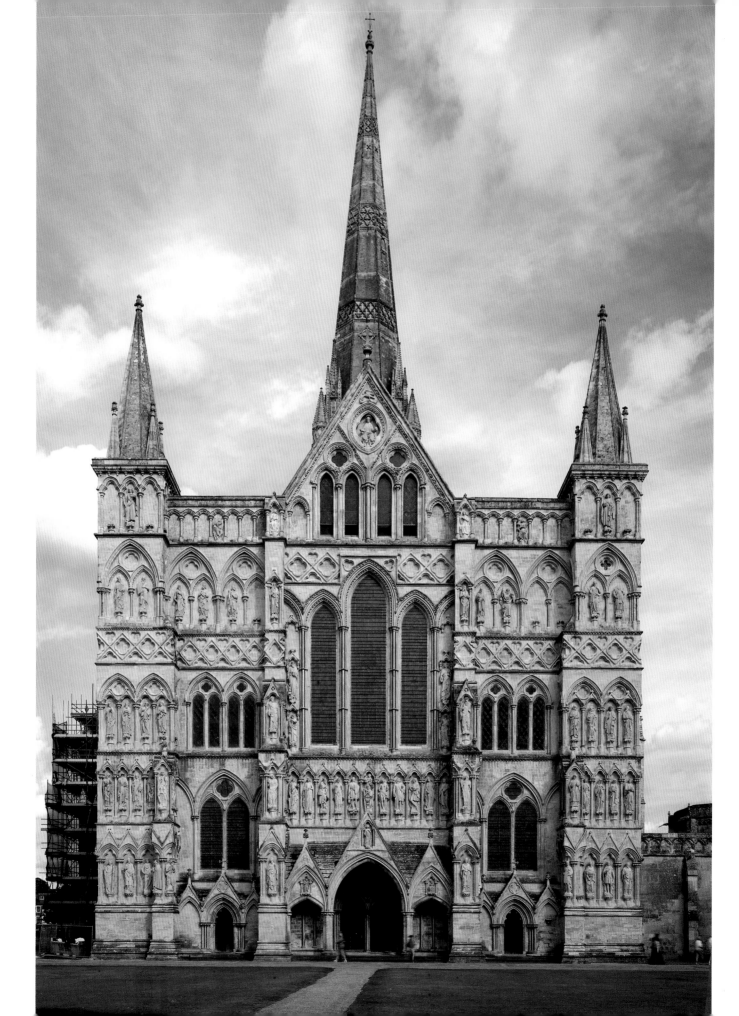

The English Screen Facade

English cathedrals differ from those of Continental Europe in several respects. While French cathedrals sprung directly from the maze of medieval streets and alleys, their English counterparts were sited just outside the city walls. An English cathedral was commonly a freestanding building set in a grassy precinct known as the cathedral close. The idyllic setting contributed to the romantic aura that still surrounds English churches and cathedrals today.

The cathedral close is not the only distinctly English feature a visitor might notice. In Germany or France, a facade with two towers was the norm. In England, however, broad, decorated screen facades were the rule, a dazzling stage curtain in front of the nave with no structural logic. The west portal, an important site for sculpture in French churches, received next to no figural decoration in the English version. The main entrance to an English cathedral was canonically on the northeastern side, entered through a magnificently decorated vestibule. The unique quality of English cathedrals is nowhere more apparent than in Salisbury Cathedral, where the portals are distinctly undersized in relation to the overall dimensions of the facade.

One of the most beautiful screen facades is that of Wells Cathedral, completed between 1230 and 1240. The facade is a masterpiece of architectural relief sculpture covered with a network of blind arches. The screen facade of Peterborough Cathedral, while decorated with statues of saints, has three deep, relatively undecorated portals that look back to the Romanesque period.

Above: **Peterborough,** cathedral,
west facade, 1180–1238.

Right: **Wells,** cathedral,
west facade, 1230–1240.

Opposite: **Salisbury,** cathedral,
west facade, begun 1220.

Westminster Abbey and the Decorated Style

Westminster Abbey marks the second phase of English Gothic: the decorated style. There are good reasons for this name. Between 1240 and 1330 the building arts took off in a number of experimental directions, primarily in terms of decoration. Every surface would be ornamented, from walls and windows to columns and vaults, with decoration taking precedence over structural innovation. The London abbey church in Westminster became the prototype for the new style. King Henry III built what is today better known as Westminster Abbey for political reasons. He wanted to compete with the cathedrals of the great cities of France, and it is therefore not surprising that Westminster Abbey is the most "French" building of the English Gothic. Its architect was Henry of Reyns, his name indicating that he probably came from Reims. Reims is a northern French city with a famously decorative cathedral to which some aspects of Westminster Abbey bear a particularly close resemblance. The layout of the choir is entirely French, as are the apsidal chapels and the elevation of the nave. The nave rises to a height of almost 105 feet (32 m), unusually tall for England, and unimaginable without the influence of Reims.

Lincoln Cathedral's Angel Choir represents a further development in the decorated style. Instead of a closed divider, the eastern wall of the choir is pierced with elaborate traceried windows.

Above and right: **London,** Westminster Abbey, nave from the west; ground plan; facade.

Westminster Abbey

Opposite: **Lincoln,** cathedral, showing the typically English square end of the Angel Choir, 1256–1280.

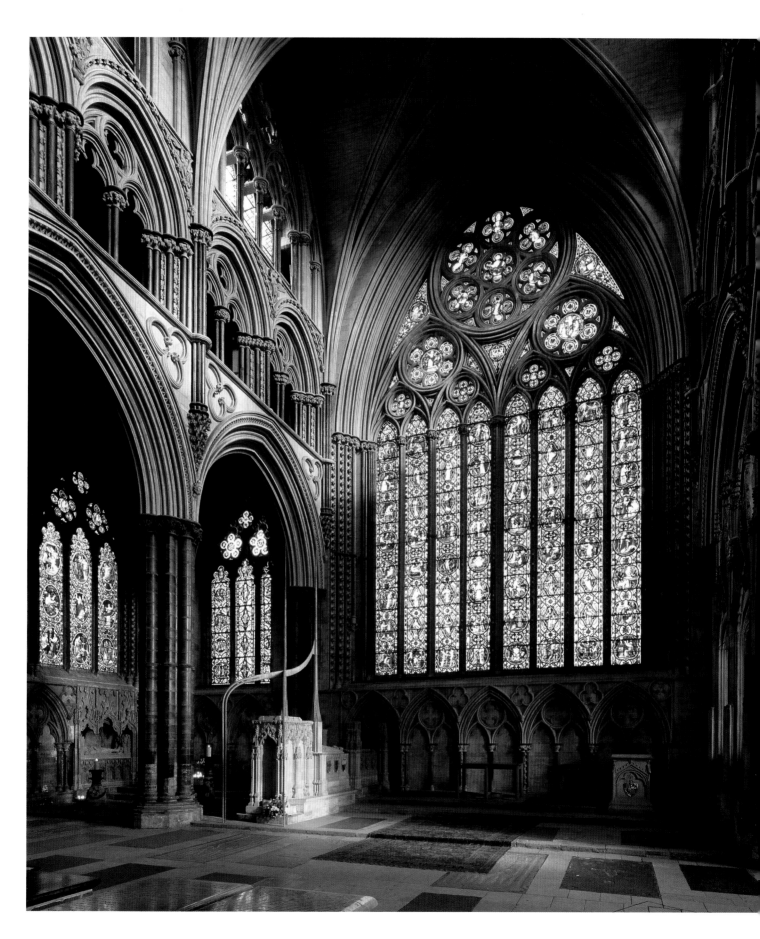

Gloucester Cathedral and the Perpendicular Style

The wall decor of Gloucester Cathedral belongs to the third style of English Gothic architecture, the perpendicular style, which came into its own from 1330. While no less aesthetically motivated than the decorated style, perpendicular-style cathedrals can be viewed as a reaction to its excessive manifestations. The new style is organized around vertical and horizontal linear elements; slender panels form a delicate latticework that both adorn and unify. The visual and structural advantages of the new style are visible in the east window of Gloucester Cathedral's choir: the latticed window occupies nearly the entire wall, conveying lightness and grace.

Gloucester, cathedral, choir, ca. 1337–1360. Grave monument of Edward II, 1330–1335 (opposite). The murdered king's monument is executed in white alabaster and dark Purbeck marble. The noble countenance of the image does not betray the inglorious circumstances of his death.

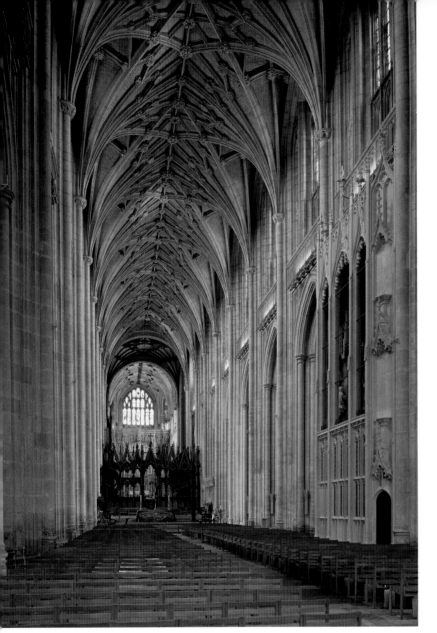

Winchester Cathedral and King's College Chapel, Cambridge

The perpendicular style spread like wildfire, in part because its basic canon of forms was so easily and inexpensively adapted to a variety of buildings. During the fourteenth century, both Canterbury and Winchester were given new naves in the perpendicular style. Winchester Cathedral, however, is an exception in many ways. Its facade and plan, begun in 1360, are closer to those of Continental churches than the more typical English cathedral. Once begun, construction ground to a halt after just six years. In 1394, Bishop William Wykeham hired William Wynford to chisel perpendicular elements into the massive, Romanesque walls of the nave. This unusual treatment was probably a decision motivated by financial pressures. Despite his very fine work, the massiveness of the walls still comes through.

While cathedrals were dominant in the development of the Gothic during the thirteenth and fourteenth centuries, colleges began to take on this role in the fifteenth. Kings College Chapel in Cambridge is one of the most beautiful sacred spaces ever built. It is justly famous for its gossamer tracery, refined wall shafts, and breathtaking fan vaulting. The chapel was founded in 1446 by Henry IV, with plans provided by building master Reginald of Ely, who directed construction and designed the unique vaults. Architect John Wastell would complete the vaulting in the sixteenth century.

Above and right: **Winchester,** cathedral, nave, 1360–1404, and facade, 1360–1366. The Romanesque nave was reworked in the perpendicular style by master mason William Wynford.

Opposite: **Cambridge,** King's College Chapel, 1416–1515. King's College Chapel is both the culmination and the end of English Gothic architecture.

Assisi, interior view of the upper church
S. Francesco (St Francis), 1228–1253.
Frescoes by Giotto (ca. 1295) show scenes
from the life of St Francis.

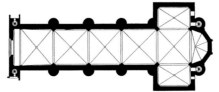

Above: **Bologna,** S. Francesco,
1236–1256, central nave with chevet
in the background.

Above: **Todi,** interior of S. Fortunato,
1292–1328. Slender column shafts
decorate the piers.

Churches of the Italian Mendicant Orders

The Franciscan and Dominican orders brought Gothic to
Italy. The double church above the grave of St Francis of
Assisi was begun in 1228 and consecrated in 1253. The
refined taste evident throughout the church reflects the
Franciscan's new ideas about piety and religious expression, which involve a life full of work governed by
personal humility and a total rejection of worldly power
in all its manifestations. The upper church of S. Francesco became the model for all later sacred architecture
in Italy. The broad, two-storied nave is structurally simple,
with massive walls pierced by windows that flood the
interior with light. Slender clustered columns support

the ribbing of the square nave bays. Although the model
for early Italian Gothic is clearly France, the overall
impression of S. Francesco is very different than that of
any contemporary French church.

The high-relief screen facade of the Franciscan abbey church in Bologna conceals a three-story building
with a Cistercian-style chevet. S. Fortunato in Todi has a
light-filled interior with no clear point of focus, capped
by a broad expanse of finely ribbed vaulting. The lighter
elements of the new Gothic seem to have made its
builders a little nervous. During construction, transverse
arches were added to the side aisles for extra support.

Opposite and above: **Florence,**
S. Croce, begun 1294, interior
(above) and view of the main choir
chapel (opposite), with frescos by
Agnolo Gaddi (after 1374).

Above: **Florence,** S. Maria Novella,
begun 1246, interior view.

Churches of the Mendicant Orders in Florence

The Franciscans and Dominicans ensured that Italian Gothic architecture had a distinctive look. While Cistercian monasteries were tucked into remote valleys, mendicant orders sought contact with the people they served. Franciscan and Dominican monasteries were built on the outskirts of cities, with spacious churches to accommodate large crowds of worshippers. Most had straightforward plans with well-defined structural elements. Architectural decor was kept simple, used only when necessary. Instead, the extensive wall surfaces were filled with narrative frescoes, which, in addition to the monks' sermons, served to instruct the laity.

The Dominican Abbey Church of S. Maria Novella (begun 1246) was a milestone. It follows the Cistercian model of a three-aisled nave with a transept and square chapels and choir, but the articulation of the interior space reveals distinct differences between Cistercian designs and the Italian Gothic. Where Cistercian designs rely on sharp divisions, the almost 340-foot (100-m) long nave of S. Maria Novella uses slender piers enhanced by

attached half-columns to create a more rhythmic transition between the nave and side aisles. Also new is the use of alternating light and gray-green sandstone blocks in the arches. The striped effect makes the otherwise static support element dynamic, blurring the line of spatial transition.

In 1294, the Franciscans gave Florence the stunning S. Croce. Its dimensions were meant to surpass those of S. Maria Novella the nave is 377 feet (115 m) long, the transept 242 feet (74 m) wide, and the nave roof 125 feet (38 m) tall—it would have towered over contemporary French cathedrals. The large scale was not entirely due to a desire for self-promotion. The Franciscans wanted a church large enough to become the preferred burial site for the wealthy of Florence, providing them with a final opportunity to express their humility. In this, S. Croce was wildly successful. The banking families of Bardi, Peruzzi, and Alberti left behind stunning chapels adorned with fresco cycles by Giotto, Gaddi, and other artists, wonders that still draw visitors today.

Top and above: **Florence,** cathedral, begun 1294, facade completed 1875–1887. View of the baptistery, church, and bell tower (top); and interior (above).

Right: **Florence,** cathedral, bell tower, begun 1334 by Giotto, taken over after his death by Andrea Pisano and Francesco Talenti, who completed the tower.

Florence Cathedral

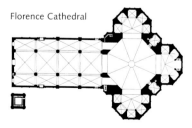

Cathedrals in Florence and Siena

The Northern Italian city-states were constantly engaged in a battle for prestige, a contest in which the majesty of their churches and cathedrals played no small role. Siena Cathedral is a prime example of the consequences of overreaching expectations and the inevitable failure that follows in their wake. In the course of an extensive renovation of the city's Romanesque cathedral, the decision was made to insert an enormous crossing with a massive dome. The final version of the plan called for an even bolder redesign, in which the old cathedral became the transept of an otherwise entirely new construction. Grave errors in the engineering of this ambitious project led to its being

abandoned in 1355. Despite its incomplete state, the overall homogeneity of what stands today is striking. Gothic and Romanesque parts of the building were clad, inside and out, in bands of black and white marble to provide a sense of visual unity.

The new cathedral in Florence was much more successful. Rich local patrons began construction of this *opus plurimum sumptuosum* in 1296, with the earliest plan provided by architect Arnolfo di Cambio. Work slowed to a halt following his death, until Giotto was named building master. He focused his attention almost entirely on the bell tower. Work on the cathedral building itself did not resume until 1357 after Francesco Talenti presented a model of an enormous rib vaulted nave with the most gigantic crossing dome yet conceived. The nave, with

Siena, cathedral, begun mid-12th century, rebuilt in the 13th and 14th centuries. The facade by Giovanni Pisano was begun 1284–1296 and completed 1357.

its 131-foot (40-m) high bays, was completed in 1378, with the crossing piers following twenty years later. In 1420, Filippo Brunelleschi took over the design and engineering of the ambitious dome. His brilliant solution was a double-shell construction that was one of the first architectural masterpieces of the Early Renaissance.

Below and opposite top: **Orvieto,** cathedral, begun 1290, interior and facade ca. 1300 by Siena architect Lorenzo Maitani. Work continued under the supervision of Andrea Pisano and Andrea Orcagna during the mid-14th century.

Orvieto Cathedral

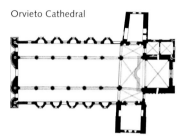

Orvieto Cathedral

Like Siena Cathedral, Orvieto Cathedral is a Romanesque building that was substantially rebuilt in Gothic style. The cathedral houses an important relic, the *sacro corporale*, an altar cloth stained with the blood of Christ from a Host that miraculously started bleeding during mass. The cloth was housed in a sumptuously decorated late Gothic reliquary shrine.

The facade of the cathedral resembles a shrine, with its opulently detailed portals, gables, towers and finials. Like a reliquary shrine, the walls in between the architectural details are filled with richly sculpted and painted pictorial decoration. The level of detail is high, giving an oddly precious impression, particularly in comparison to the generous proportions of the interior spaces.

The facade follows plans by Lorenzo Maitani, whose design replaced an earlier and simpler plan with a single gable. Both plans can be viewed at the cathedral complex today.

Pisa, S. Maria della Spina

Except for the scale of it, the Church of S. Maria della Spina could also be mistaken for an elaborate reliquary. In fact, it was the acquisition by the city of a splinter of the Crown of Thorns in 1333 that spurred the expansion of the pre-existing chapel on the site.

The architecture makes clear reference to the Sainte-Chapelle in France, where the rest of the Crown of Thorns is kept. The side elevations, which interweave gables, finials, and window tracery, follow the French model closely, with decorative elements fully integrated into the structure of the building. The main facade, with its indentations and projections, is also sculptural both in conception and execution. The delicate proportions of the Pisa church are something completely its own, and integral to its enduring allure.

Right: **Pisa,** S. Maria della Spina, 1323–1333. This marble building was relocated during the 19th century due to the threat of flooding.

Milan Cathedral

With its five aisled nave, three aisled transept, and enormous chevet, Milan cathedral is one of the largest Christian churches ever built. The most renowned architects of the day were involved in its planning, engineering, and construction, among them the Parler family and Ulrich von Ensingen. In the end, it was the design of Italian architect and mathematician Gabriele Stornaloco that had the most influence on the cathedral's final form. The exterior of the cathedral was only completed in the nineteenth century.

Bologna, S. Petronio

Just four years after Milan's cathedral was begun, the citizens of Bologna were presented with a wooden model that, had it been executed as planned, would have left all previous churches in its shadow. The parish church of S. Petronio was planned as a three-aisled basilica of gargantuan dimensions. Its nave would extend 612 feet (182 m), with its transept almost 450 feet (137 m) wide. Its enormous dome was intended to be wider and taller than the one in Florence. The interior, which was relatively plain com-

Opposite and above:
Milan, cathedral, begun 1387, exterior completed in the 19th century. View of transept and choir (above), with late Gothic tracery windows dating from the early 15th century.

Right: **Bologna,** S. Petronio, begun ca. 1390–mid-16th century, view of the interior.

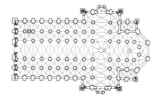

Milan Cathedral

pared to Milan Cathedral, was begun in 1390. When the church's architect, Antonio di Vicenzo, died in 1400, only two bays of the nave were complete, and only 65 feet (20 m) had been vaulted. In 1525, the remaining bays were completed and the north facade begun. The transept and choir would never be built.

Although only bits and pieces of the original plan were realized, S. Petronio remains the high point of Tuscan and Lombard sacred architecture. Its unique breadth, elegant simplicity, and the aesthetics of its material make it a worthy example of Italy's exceptional, creative interpretation of Gothic architecture.

Burgos Cathedral

The thirteenth century in Spain began with the arrival of Gothic influences from France. Bishop Mauricio von Burgo, who had been a student in Paris and was familiar with current trends in cathedral architecture, played a key role in its acceptance. In 1221, he commissioned a new Gothic cathedral for his home city of Burgos. The choir, along with many other details, was a near-copy of France's Bourges Cathedral. Burgos Cathedral was completed within just nine years.

Afterwards, late Gothic elements were introduced at Burgos. The two facade towers were erected between 1442 and 1458, both with pierced steeples resembling the cathedrals in Ulm and Esslingen. Unsurprisingly, their architect was the German Hans of Cologne, called Juan Colonia in Spain. His son Simon designed and engineered the cathedral's famous Capilla del Condestable, the chapel reserved for the use of local dignitaries. It is a masterpiece of architectural decoration. The finely detailed crossing tower was completed by Juan de Vallejo in 1567. It integrates flamboyant structural details with Islamic decorative motifs, and openwork star vaults that are the height of artistic and technical perfection.

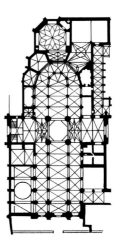

Opposite: **Burgos,** cathedral, begun 1221. The facade was reconstructed in the 18th and 19th centuries. Important late Gothic elements include the facade towers by Hans of Cologne (Juan Colonia), constructed from 1442 to 1458, and the *cimborrio* (crossing tower) by Juan de Vallejo (1567).

Above: Interior of the *cimborrio* with its magnificent star vaulting.

Toledo Cathedral

With its five aisles, double chevet, and ring of what were once fifteen chapels, Toledo Cathedral is one of the largest Spanish buildings of the thirteenth century. As the seat of an archbishop, it occupies the highest rank of all cathedrals in Spain. Begun in 1222, its architect Martín was strongly influenced by Bourges Cathedral in France, but also sought to go beyond it by integrating Islamic elements with its French Gothic structure. The triforium, for example, includes arabesque arches.

León Cathedral

León Cathedral was originally planned as yet another synthesis of French rayonnant architecture. Its ambitious design incorporates aspects of the royal cathedral of Reims, the royal mausoleum at St Denis, and even the royal Sainte-Chapelle in Paris. The bar could hardly have been set any higher, although León itself was of no particular religious or political status. The French aspects of the interior include nearly completely preserved stained glass windows that fill the room with wondrous, colored light.

Above: **Toledo,** cathedral, begun 1222, choir ambulatory with arabesque arches in the triforium.

Right and opposite: **León,** cathedral, begun 1255. Exterior (right) and detail of the nave and stained glass windows, 13th through 16th centuries (opposite).

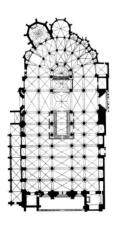

Toledo Cathedral

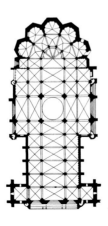

León Cathedral

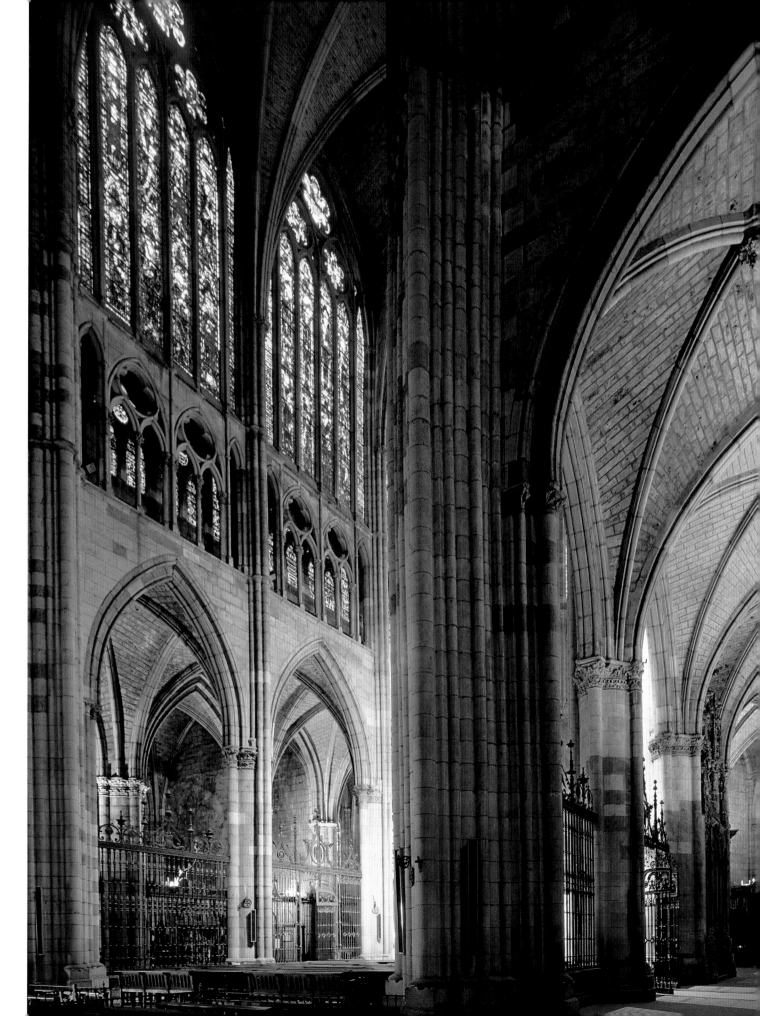

Palma de Mallorca Cathedral

Anyone approaching the island city of Palma de Mallorca by sea is greeted by the unforgettable sight of the cathedral's silhouette on the horizon. Its defiant profile is supported by a system of integrated, massive, closely spaced brace walls and piers. The artful arrangement of structural elements gives the almost 350-foot (110-m) long walls a graphic quality, like latticework. The nave, raised in 1369, is 138 feet (42 m) and three stories high and has exceptionally slender columns and piers. The overwhelming interior is comparable to that of the cathedrals in Bourges, Beauvais, and Milan. Catalan architect Berenguer de Montagut was likely responsible for the design.

Barcelona Cathedral

Barcelona Cathedral began construction in 1298 under the direction of architect Jaume Fabre. It is one of the most imposing monuments of Catalonian Gothic architecture. Its broad nave with side aisles of almost the same height combine to create a magnificent interior space. Massive compound piers divide the nave bays. The colored vault keystones, however, date from a later period of construction (1448). The crypt was completed in 1337, likely still under the direction of the original architect. The twelve-part fan vaults, also his work, inspired twentieth century architect Antoni Gaudí in his design for La Sagrada Familia.

Opposite top left and bottom: **Palma de Mallorca,** cathedral, begun ca. 1300, exterior (bottom) and interior, begun 1369.

Opposite top right: **Barcelona,** interior of Sta. Maria del Mar, begun 1329, consecrated 1384.

Above and below: **Barcelona,** cathedral, begun 1298, interior (above) and crypt with marble sarcophagus of Sta. Eulàlia (below), 1327–1339.

Barcelona, Sta. Maria del Mar

Merchants and sailors contributed to the construction of Sta. Maria del Mar. Its first architect was Berenguer de Montagut, followed by Ramon Despuig and Guillem Metge, who died before the church was consecrated in 1384. Like most churches of the Catalonian Gothic, Sta. Maria del Mar has a simple, though finely finished, exterior. The facades are barely distinguished, giving no hint that some of the most magnificent Gothic interiors ever built lie behind them. There is also considerable decorative restraint inside the church, with plain octagonal piers supporting the vaulting. The plan is well within the Catalan tradition with its three aisle nave, unaccentuated transept, side aisles that continue around the choir, and chapels set between the wall buttresses.

The nave is exceptionally wide at 46 feet (14 m), and was something of a sensation in its day. Only the dome of the cathedral in Girona spans a greater distance.

Seville Cathedral

Seville Cathedral is, in many ways, the building that most embodies the political, cultural, and architectural trends of the late medieval period in Spain. Erected on the foundations of an old mosque, the plan of the cathedral both adopts and transcends Islamic spatial relationships with a Gothic superstructure that visually proclaims the triumph of the western world. Architectural decoration follows a similar dichotomy. Moorish brickwork dominates inside and out, while exterior support elements of European Gothic origin appear here on a large scale for the first time in Spain. Spanish Gothic reaches its ultimate expression in this combination of traditional Gothic elements with the closed plan common in Catalonian and Aragonese sacred architecture.

Seville Cathedral was the work of a number of architects, most of them from outside Spain. Simon of Cologne (Simon Colonia) was involved in the design of the massive crossing tower. Completed in 1506, it collapsed just five years later. Juan Gil de Hontañón took over in 1515. He is responsible for the exuberant, flamboyantly detailed vaulting.

Salamanca Cathedral

While St Peter's in Rome was introducing the classicizing style of the High Renaissance to Europe, in Spain cathedrals continued to be built in late Gothic manner. Spanish architects' loyalty to the principles of Gothic architecture is not necessarily evidence of their backwardness; there was some regionalism involved as well. Gothic architecture was called *moderno* (modern) in Spain, while the Renaissance forms were referred to as *romano* (Roman), a reference to their classical elements as well as to geopolitical associations of buildings in that style.

The golden age of Spanish late Gothic architecture began with the construction of Astorga Cathedral, by Juan Gil de Hontañón. His design became the basis for the new cathedral built in Salamanca shortly afterward. Its skeletal Gothic structure creates a monumental exterior with generously proportioned interiors. The net vaults are among the most magnificent ever produced in an architectural style with a propensity for taking structural elements, and making them beautiful.

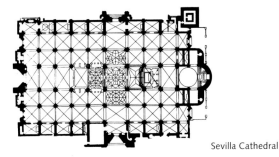

Sevilla Cathedral

Left and opposite bottom: **Seville,** cathedral, 1402–1506, view from the southwest, with the Giralda Tower, completed in 1198, in background.

Opposite top: **Salamanca,** New Cathedral, begun 1513. The Romanesque Old Cathedral is visible in the foreground.

Batalha, Monastery of S. Maria da
Vitoria, begun 1385, completed 1533.
Below: Claustro Real (Royal Cloister),
late 14th century. Right: nave. Bottom:
The Capela do Fundador (Founders
Chapel), with the Capela Imperfeita
(Imperfect Chapel) to the east.

Batalha, S. Maria da Vitoria

Portugal has just one building dating to the early Gothic period: the Cistercian Abbey in Alobaca. Late Gothic architecture can be seen in the Dominican Abbey church of S. Maria da Vitoria in Batalha. It was commissioned by João I after a victory over the Castilians in 1385, and completed in the sixteenth century. The plans were the work of Afonso Domingues, who directed the construction of the three aisled nave and transept from 1388 to 1402. The building was then taken over by a certain Master Hueget, who was probably an Englishman. His most important contributions are the two mausoleums: the square Capela do Fundador (Founders Chapel), and the circular Royal Chapel. The latter remained unfinished, and is therefore known as the Capela Imperfeita (Imperfect Chapel).

Belém, Mosteiro dos Jerónimos (Jerónimos Monastery)

The Hieronymite monastery in Belém, near Lisbon, is an architectural masterpiece dating to the reign of Manuel I. Designed to house the graves of the Aviz dynasty, the monastery's architecture combines late Gothic structure with elaborate, sculptural decoration symbolizing Manuel's dynastic ambitions. The result is a monumental building, unmistakably Portuguese.

Diogo Boytac designed a broad, three aisled hall church with transept and high choir. The structural details and unique vault, which spans the entire space, are the work of João de Castilho. Just six octagonal piers covered in Renaissance-style decoration support the complex net vaulting, which spans nearly 82 feet (25 m). This leaves the transept fully open, with no support elements to interrupt the space. De Castilho's engineering was so advanced that the monastery was one of very few buildings to survive the catastrophic Lisbon earthquake of 1755.

Right: **Belém (near Lisbon),**
Mosteiro dos Jerónimos, interior of the church and vaulting, 1517.

RENAISSANCE

The rebirth of antiquity, its "renaissance," had its origins in early fifteenth-century Italy, and architecture played a key role. In 1414, the ancient text *de Architectura* was rediscovered. This ten-volume collection of classical building principles and techniques was the work of Vitruvius, an ancient Roman architect and engineer who lived in the first century BCE. Although it was not illustrated, the text brought about a revolution. From then on, architects and patrons were inspired by ancient Greece and Rome; medieval and especially Gothic styles were considered overwrought. They were supplanted by an ideal rooted in ancient systems of balanced, harmonious proportions: a perfect building should mirror the proportions of the ideal human form. Vitruvius' four architectural orders—Doric, Ionic, Corinthian, and Tuscan—remained essential formal elements of every building well into the nineteenth century. The spread of the new architecture was greatly facilitated by the relatively new technology of the printing press. Architectural manifestos by Leone Battista Alberti, Vignola, Sebastiano Serlio, and Andrea Palladio carried the ideas of the Italian Renaissance all over the known world.

Sacred architecture remained the most prestigious type of building. Two Florentine basilicas, S. Lorenzo and S. Spirito, both by Filippo Brunelleschi, mark the birth of Renaissance architecture. Brunelleschi provided the new style with its own syntax and formal expression. His design for the 148-feet (46-m) dome of Florence Cathedral was a bravura technical achievement; like so much Renaissance innovation, it was thought impossible just a few years before.

Leone Battista Alberti was above all a theoretician. He found the longstanding Latin cross plan anachronistic, and instead favored plans based on the ideal geometric forms of circle, square, hexagon, and octagon. The facade of the Tempio Malatestiano, actually a Franciscan church, and later the front of S. Andrea in Mantua, were dramatically reconceived as ancient Roman triumphal arches. The application of motifs that were originally pagan to churches did not hamper the growing influence of antiquity-influenced architecture. The proof is plain to see in Christianity's most important "temple," St Peter's in Rome, itself a triumphal monument to Michelangelo's artistry and skill.

At the turn of the fifteenth century to the sixteenth, Florence's status as seat of innovation and patron of the new art and architecture came to an end; Rome dominated the High Renaissance. In 1496, Michelangelo moved to the city on the Tiber, followed by Bramante in 1499 and Raphael in 1508. The ancient monuments could be studied onsite in Rome as they could not be in Florence, and Pope Julius II had an ambitious vision of rebuilding Rome and returning it to its former glory as *caput mundi* (capital of the world). For the next two hundred years, Rome used architecture to support its claims of political and religious pre-eminence. Even the tensions that led to the Reformation in much of Europe strengthened Rome's position. The Counter Reformation and its chief promulgators, the Jesuits, proclaimed a new understanding of religion, images, and buildings that spread Rome's influence as far away as the New World.

Whether "Renaissance" rightly applies to fifteenth and sixteenth century architecture outside Italy remains controversial. Northern European architects copied ancient models only superficially, if at all, and classical details were sprinkled throughout what were essentially still late Gothic structures. No effort was made to incorporate the Italian theoreticians' concept of a building as the physical expression of thought. On the other hand, this mixture of old and new stylistic directions produced some of the most creative buildings ever constructed.

Rome, St Peter's, western apse, Michelangelo Buonarotti, begun 1558. Colossal double pilasters give the walls plasticity and volume.

Left: *Vitruvian Man,* Leonardo da Vinci, late 15th century.

Opposite: **Rimini,** Chapel of S. Sigismondo in Tempio Malatestiano (S. Francesco), Leone Battista Alberti (architect) and Agostino di Duccio (sculptor), begun 1446.

Pablo de la Riestra
A Typical Renaissance Church Building

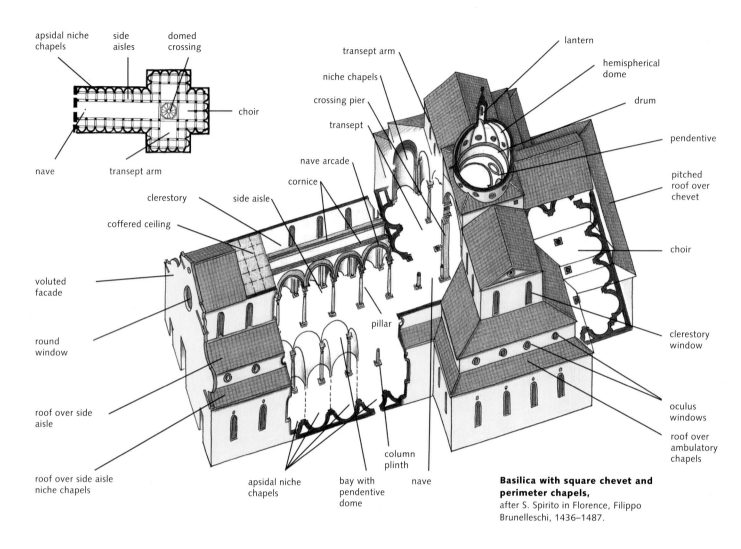

apsidal niche chapels

side aisles

domed crossing

choir

nave

transept arm

transept arm

niche chapels

crossing pier

transept

nave arcade

cornice

clerestory

side aisle

coffered ceiling

voluted facade

round window

roof over side aisle

roof over side aisle niche chapels

apsidal niche chapels

bay with pendentive dome

column plinth

nave

pillar

lantern

hemispherical dome

drum

pendentive

pitched roof over chevet

choir

clerestory window

oculus windows

roof over ambulatory chapels

Basilica with square chevet and perimeter chapels,
after S. Spirito in Florence, Filippo Brunelleschi, 1436–1487.

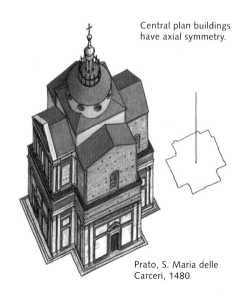

Central plan buildings have axial symmetry.

Prato, S. Maria delle Carceri, 1480

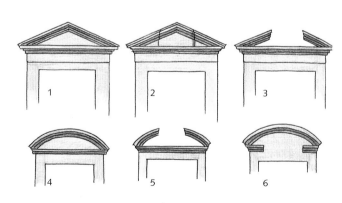

Gables for windows and doors

1 triangular pediment

2 triangular pediment, sectioned

3 triangular pediment, broken at top

4 segmented pediment

5 segmented pediment, broken at top

6 segmented pediment, broken at base

Renaissance to Mannerism
Axonometric projection with plan, interior and exterior elevations

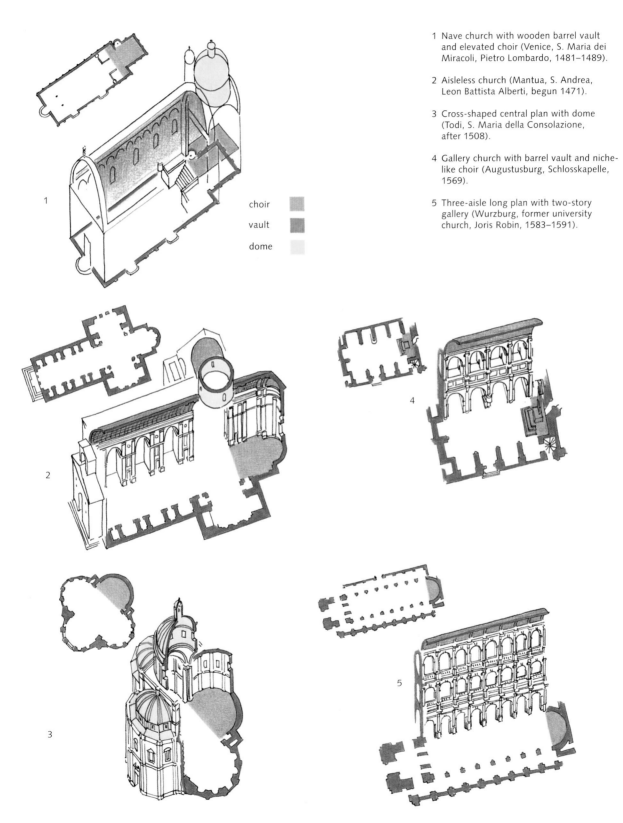

choir
vault
dome

1 Nave church with wooden barrel vault and elevated choir (Venice, S. Maria dei Miracoli, Pietro Lombardo, 1481–1489).

2 Aisleless church (Mantua, S. Andrea, Leon Battista Alberti, begun 1471).

3 Cross-shaped central plan with dome (Todi, S. Maria della Consolazione, after 1508).

4 Gallery church with barrel vault and niche-like choir (Augustusburg, Schlosskapelle, 1569).

5 Three-aisle long plan with two-story gallery (Wurzburg, former university church, Joris Robin, 1583–1591).

Brunelleschi and the Early Renaissance

The work of Filippo Brunelleschi served as an incubator not only for the Early Renaissance, but for all new architecture in Italy and Europe. Structurally, his buildings are physical manifestations of rationalism and clarity. Formal elements are simple, with clearly demarcated horizontal and vertical lines, carefully considered proportions, and symmetrical elevations for an overall impression of complete harmony. Brunelleschi's churches revive the Early Christian basilica plan, transforming it into something utterly new with the imposition of a mathematically precise system of formal proportions and spatial relationships.

Brunelleschi's surface treatments are dominated by the alternation of white and greenish courses of marble. These are both a decorative accent and conscious emphasis calling attention to the masonry and engineering. Many of these elements were already present in the eleventh century. The classical details and marble incrustation in the new Florentine buildings were clearly inspired by local Romanesque buildings in the medieval style often referred to as "Tuscan Renaissance." In the fifteenth century, however, details like these were understood as direct references to original ancient prototypes.

Brunelleschi's masterpiece is the dome of Florence Cathedral, a double shell construction strengthened by ribbing. It was erected without any support from central scaffolding.

Above left and right: **Florence,** S. Spirito, Filippo Brunelleschi, begun 1436, interior; sacristy by Il Cronaca and others, 1488.

Below: **Florence,** cathedral, dome, Filippo Brunelleschi, begun 1420. Opposite: **Florence,** S. Lorenzo, Filippo Brunelleschi, begun 1420, interior.

Right: **Florence,** S. Maria Novella, Leone Battista Alberti, begun 1458, facade with inlaid marble decoration.

Opposite and below: **Mantua,** S. Andrea, Leone Battista Alberti, begun 1472, interior and facade with triumphal arch.

Florence, S. Maria Novella

After Brunelleschi, the most important figure in the Early Italian Renaissance is the humanist philosopher, artist, and diplomat Leone Battista Alberti (1401–1472). His treatise *De Re Aedificatoria* (1451) is the first of many theoretical works scrutinizing the forms and functions of architecture, and his renovation of the facade of S. Maria Novella was aesthetically revolutionary. His use of volutes to visually minimize the height difference between the narrower, taller nave and the wider but lower side aisles was an elegant device that would be copied in countless fifteenth and sixteenth century churches.

Mantua, S. Andrea

Alberti's design for S. Andrea in Mantua (1470) pointed the way for the High Renaissance. Like Brunelleschi's Pazzi Chapel, or his own Tempio Malatestiano, S. Andrea's facade has the form of a Roman triumphal arch, here on a truly monumental scale. On the side facing the street, a triangular pediment crowns walls visually partitioned by colossal pilasters. The architectonic divisions of the facade reflect the spatial divisions of the interior. The nave is covered with a coffered barrel vault whose thrust is received by the transverse vaults of the side chapels. The interior is defined by the alternation of chapel niches and narrower wall surfaces between them. The relationship is a precisely measured 3:4 ratio developed by Alberti from his study of ancient architecture. It would become a characteristic feature of sacred architecture for the next few centuries.

Above: **Prato,** S. Maria delle Carceri, Giuliano da Sangallo, begun 1484, exterior of the Greek cross plan building.

The Central Plan in Tuscany and Umbria

During the Renaissance, the house of God was perceived as the physical manifestation of his perfection. Alberti and his contemporaries therefore favored the central plan, based as it was on basic geometric forms that were "perfect" in their symmetry. Nature herself, "the divine teacher," was thought to prefer circles, squares, octagons, Greek crosses, and their derivations. Drawings and illustrations in numerous treatises from the quattrocentro attest to just how seriously the subject was pursued. Leonardo left a complete catalog of basic geometric forms and equations. His emphasis on the role of natural proportions in the design process is evident in what is perhaps his best-known drawing: *Vitruvian Man*. In it, Leonardo aligns circles and squares within an idealized human form, and compares the measurements of a building with the proportions of the figure's outstretched arms and outspread legs. The well-built Vitruvian male is the very image of the cosmos; his physical geography and perfect proportions the very embodiment of celestial harmony. Should an architect follow this model, this harmony would naturally transfer to his own creations. There could be no better system for the design of sacred buildings.

While most of Leonardo's own architecture stayed on paper, centrally planned buildings sprung up everywhere, often outside the big cities. One of the most influential, and loveliest, is the Church of S. Maria delle Carceri in Prato, a Greek cross central plan building designed by Giuliano da Sangallo sometime after 1484. S. Maria della Consolazione in Todi is another. Thought to be based on the ideas of either Leonardo or Bramante, the four arms of its central cross terminate in apses. The Todi church and the church in Biagio bei Montepulciano (begun 1518) share yet another common idea, one promoted in Alberti's treatises. All very deliberately resemble temples, and as such stand out from the hustle and bustle of everyday life.

Left: **Montepulciano,** S. Biagio, Antonio da Sangallo and others, 1518–1540. Bramante's design for St Peter's in Rome is a clear influence.

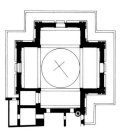

Prado, S. Maria delle Carceri

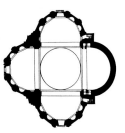

Todi, S. Maria della Consolazione

Opposite: **Todi,** S. Maria della Consolazione, Baldassare Peruzzi and Cola da Caprarola, begun 1508, exterior view.

with a certain monumentality and plasticity of form balanced against the proportions of the monastery courtyard enclosing the site. The Doric order controlling the lower story is archaeologically accurate.

Bramante's Tempietto represents a culmination of quattrocentro experimentation with the central plan. In uniting the form of a pagan temple with a shrine to a Christian martyr, it serves as an important symbol of historical continuity within the Roman Church.

Below: **Milan,** S. Maria delle Grazie, Donato Bramante, begun 1492.

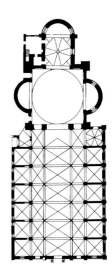

Milan, S. Maria delle Grazie

Opposite and above: **Rome,** S. Pietro in Montorio, Tempietto, Donato Bramante, begun 1502, a classically authentic centrally planned building, exterior and interior.

Milan, S. Maria delle Grazie

Donato di Pascussio d'Antonio (1444-1514), called Bramante, devoted his life to the design and construction of centrally planned buildings. One of the masterpieces of his early period in Milan was the new construction of S. Satiro, where space was so tight that the coffered ceiling had to be painted on! In S. Maria delle Grazie (begun 1492), in contrast, a genuine, massive dome rises over the triconch choir. Bramante played with geometric forms, creating a hierarchy of scale that was recognizable in his later works, as well. Plans for the new St Peter's in Rome seem to have had their origins in Milan.

Rome, S. Pietro in Montorio, Tempietto

The Tempietto (little temple) in the courtyard of S. Pietro in Montorio is Bramante's first completed work in Rome, the city that would serve as the incubator of the "classic" High Renaissance. The Tempietto is a small memorial building commissioned by Ferdinand and Isabella, the king and queen of Spain. It is said to mark the spot where St Peter the Apostle was crucified. Begun in 1560 when Bramante was already sixty years old, the Tempietto comes closer to the ancient ideal than any earlier building. Although of modest size, Bramante infused its proportions

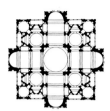

Donato Bramante,
1506

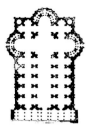

Raffael, 1514

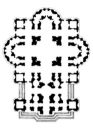

Antonio da Sangallo
the Younger, 1539

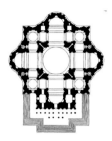

Michelangelo, 1546

Left, below and opposite:
Rome, St Peter's, begun 1506,
plans by different architects;
exterior; and view of Michelangelo's great dome.

Rome, St Peter's

In 1506, Pope Julius II decided to replace the increasingly de-crepit St Peter with a worthy new building. While previous popes had been content to expand and renovate the old basilica, Julius II was inspired to initiate a monumental new building in the contemporary style. He wanted a building that would serve as a beacon of the Roman Catholic Church, proclaiming its glory, and that of its pope, to the entire world. Only the grave of St Peter would remain untouched, its site given a new prominence inside the great building that would rise up around it. Work began in April 1508 following a plan by Bramante with assistance from Giuliano da Sangallo. This plan, filed in the Uffizi Gallery today as Plan 1A, called for a three-aisled central plan over a Greek cross. Bramante described it as "combining the Pantheon with Constantine's basilica." Although the project was never completed in this form, the basic formula survived through all subsequent redesigns, including the massive dome built by Michelangelo.

By the time of Bramante's death in 1514, only the 148-foot (45-m) tall triumphal arch of the crossing had been built. He was succeeded by Raphael, who accepted what was there, but modified Bramante's design by adding a long nave with side chapels. Raphael died suddenly in 1520 and work on the new church ground to a halt. Eventually, Baldassare Peruzzi took over the project, reverting almost entirely to Bramante's original plan. Next was Antonio da Sangallo, who preferred Raphael's ap-proach. Progress was fitful, but at da Sangallo's death in 1546, the vaults for the southern and eastern transept arms and the grotto for the papal burial vaults were completed. The latter was designed to solve the problem of the elevation differences on the

sloping site of the Vatican Hill, and to provide a collection site for potentially damaging groundwater.

In late 1546, seventy-one year old Michelangelo became the new, unpaid master of the project. The aging genius reverted to Bramante's original ideas, adopting the concept of a central plan, but at the same time focused and augmented the somewhat fragmented plans of his predecessors, making it more monu-mental and dynamic. Construction of the massive dome stood at the forefront of his conception, its structure based on the dome of Florence Cathedral. The design of the apses also goes back to this draft.

Michelangelo did not live to see his masterpiece completed. By the time of his death in 1564, only the drum of the dome and the walls of the cross arms had been built. Mich-elangelo's plans were finally completed in 1590 under the super-vision of his official successors, Giacomo Barozzi da Vignola, Pirro Ligorio, Giacomo della Porta, and Domenico Fontana.

The lengthy, tangled history of St Peter's and its design continued into the baroque period, which brought some not in-significant changes. Based on liturgical concepts introduced by the Counter Reformation, Pope Paul V commissioned a long nave (an eastward extension of the central plan, as St Peter's had always been oriented toward the west). The addition was com-pleted in 1626 from a design by Carlo Maderno. Three years later, Bernini started construction on the bell towers. After the first one collapsed due to engineering errors, plans for additional ones were abandoned. Nevertheless, in the face of all opposition, Bernini persisted in his magnificent vision for St Peter's, which culminated in the design and construction of St Peter's Square.

Rome, St. Peter's

Opposite: View of the crossing with bronze baldachin by Gianlorenzo Bernini, 1624–1633. The crossing piers with statue niches can be seen at the edges of the picture, with the *cathedra Petri* in the background.

Right: View into the dome designed by Michelangelo, ca. 1546.

Below: Tomb of Alexander VII, Gianlorenzo Bernini, marble and gilt bronze, 1672–1678.

Bernini's Works in St Peter's

Urban VIII was elected pope in 1623, and soon assigned Bernini the task of completing the papal church. Bernini began work on the baldachin over St Peter's grave and the main altar in early 1624. A little later, the sculptor-architect was asked to add statue niches to the massive crossing piers, transforming them into monumental reliquaries. While the form and functions of Bernini's works followed the dominant theological concepts of his time, his sculptures and architectural additions were artistically daring. The baldachin, with its monumental "Solomonic" twisted bronze columns, made reference to the original St Peter's and to Solomon's Temple in Jerusalem. The 13-foot (4-m) tall niche figures—one of which, St Longinus, was sculpted by Bernini himself—gesture dramatically toward the main relic: the throne of St Peter.

Between 1657 and 1666, the apse was transformed around the *cathedra Petri* (the throne of the apostle-pope). Bernini took this relic and transformed its context into a visionary *gesamtkunstwerk* (fusion of all arts). His two papal tombs are also exceptional products of his artistic vision. Urban VIII's monument shows the pope in his full capacity as leader of the Roman Catholic Church, seated on a throne with his hand poised in an imperial gesture. In contrast, Alexander VII is depicted humble and kneeling in the midst of allegorical figures representing justice, wisdom, brotherhood, and truth. But death is also present, in the form of a skeleton bursting out from under a magnificently sculpted shroud, brandishing a sinister hourglass.

Bergamo, Cappella Colleoni

Renaissance architecture in Lombardy followed a different set of principles from that in Tuscany. Although the basic classical structure remained, it can be difficult to find behind the richly ornamented, pictorial facade. The mausoleum of Condottiere Bartolommeo Colleoni in Bergamo is a characteristic example. Elements reminiscent of Gothic architecture, including rose windows, dwarf galleries, and tracery, are part of the same decorative program as more typically Renaissance pilasters, pediments, and medallions. The man behind this unique building was architect-sculptor Giovanni Antonio Amadeo, one of the busiest architects in northern Italy. He was involved in the construction of the Certosa in Pavia, among many other projects.

Opposite: **Bergamo,** Cappella
Colleoni at S. Maria Maggiore,
Giovanni Antonio Amadeo,
begun 1470. Mausoleum facade.

Venice, S. Maria dei Miracoli

Throughout the entire fifteenth century, Byzantine and Gothic styles lived on in the lagoon city, where the Renaissance and its ideas took hold only very slowly. The votive church of S. Maria dei Miracoli, erected to house a miraculous image of the Virgin, is a good example of just how flexibly the new ideas could be interpreted. The barrel-vaulted nave church with its classical proportions, use of pilasters, and marble incrustation is quite close to Alberti's ideal. At the same time, the delicacy and variety of decorative elements is very much in the Venetian tradition. This little jewel of a church is the work of Pietro Lombardo and his sons.

Above left and right: **Venice,**
S. Maria dei Miracoli, Pietro Lombardo
and others, 1481–1489. Exterior and
interior views.

Palladio's Venetian Churches

Antonio Palladio, born in Padua in 1508, influenced the
architecture of his own age, and many later ages, more
than anyone else. His *Four Books of Architecture* (1570)
were consulted by every serious architect. Well into the
eighteenth century, Palladio's buildings were considered
the very epitome of Renaissance style.

Although he is primarily famed for his revitaliza-
tion of the villa, Palladio also contributed a number of
innovations to the design and construction of sacred
buildings. It was Palladio who finally solved the dilemma
of how to adapt the antique temple facade into a functional, structurally integrated part of a church, a task
architects struggled with (with little success) throughout
the fourteenth century. A second issue was typological.
The round building that had long been favored by

Renaissance architectural theorists was an ideal form, but in the increasingly heated atmosphere of the Counter Reformation, it was stigmatized as pagan; a cruciform plan was demanded, which was entirely contrary to Palladio's concept of a "Christian temple." Instead, in his two Venetian churches, Il Redentore (begun 1576) and the magnificent S. Giorgio Maggiore (begun 1566), he squared the circle: in each case he overlaid the two spatial forms and articulated them with multi-layered walls. Thus the crossing is overlaid with centralizing elements, and the basilical plan is masked with a temple front.

The multi-layered facade of Il Redentore, seen from the Giudecca Canal, is pure genius. Two ancient temple fronts are overlaid to form a dramatic, curtain-like facade rising before a massive, towering dome.

Above: **Venice,**
Il Redentore on the
Giudecca Canal, Andrea
Palladio, begun 1576.

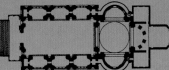

Venice, Il Redentore

Opposite, left and right: **Paris,**
St-Étienne-du-Mont, facade, begun
1610; and rood screen, ca. 1540.
This unusual, finely detailed rood
screen is one of very few of its kind
still preserved in France.

Renaissance Churches in France

France, the home of "Cathedral Gothic," adopted the new Renaissance style with difficulty. The light-filled late Gothic interiors that survive today as evidence of the perfect engineering of their vaulting, masonry, and decor, were understandably difficult to leave behind. When the Renaissance finally did make itself felt in sacred architecture, it was primarily in the form of interior decoration rather than structure. The Parisian St-Eustache, built between 1532 and 1637, has a completely Gothic plan, including a five aisle nave and double ambulatory chevet. Its decorative star vaulting is supported by slender compound piers, which are now given the shafts and capitals of classical columns. The rood screen in the Church of St-Étienne-du-Mont (before 1540?) is one of the most intriguing works in this mixed style. The screen is composed of broad, flat arches, through which one has a complete view of the east end. This is unusual, as the rood screens generally restricted that view. The elaborate structure of the St-Étienne-du-Mont rood screen was also unusual. Spiral staircases lead through it and around it on both sides, curving elegantly around the slender columns of the nave.

The facade of St Étienne-du-Mont was begun somewhat later, probably around 1610. Its style is a veritable pattern book of mannerism. Three pediments are stacked atop each other, giving the church front a decidedly vertical aspect. The lower story resembles a temple with rusticated columns, while a Gothic rose window in a segmented broken pediment occupies the center of the upper story. Mannerist motifs are also present in architect Philibert de l'Orme's design for a hunting lodge chapel in Anet (Eure-et-Loire).

In the end, the decisive step toward a new kind of sacred building in France took place in Joigny, where, from 1557 to 1596, architect Jean Chérau covered the nave of the Church of St-Jean with a broad barrel vault, thus marrying the local Romanesque tradition with the Renaissance influences arriving from Rome.

Above: **Anet Lodge,**
Philibert de l'Orme,
1547–1552, dome of the
hunting lodge chapel.

Opposite bottom and above: **Paris,**
St-Eustache, 1532–1637. Above: detail
of the clerestory, where the Gothic wall
structure is combined with Renaissance
decorative elements.

BAROQUE, ROCOCO, AND NEOCLASSICISM

Baroque and rococo styles dominate the period from the late sixteenth century through the mid-eighteenth century. This was the age of absolutism, in which princes both worldly and religious had nearly unlimited power.

The transition from Renaissance and mannerist styles to the baroque began in Rome, and the new, sensual approach to architecture was spread by artists from Rome over the course of decades. Only in the late seventeenth century did regional variations become pronounced, particularly in the Piedmont, Venice, and southern Italy, which was under Spanish rule. The papacy was the driving force behind this artistic and cultural revolution, much as it had been for the High Renaissance during the time of Michelangelo, Raphael, and Bramante; yet it was the Counter Reformation that created the ideological conditions that led to a profound transformation.

The Jesuits, in particular, exploited the rhetorical drama of baroque art to convey their beliefs to believers in the Old and New Worlds. Their first church, Il Gesù, served as a veritable incunabula of baroque sacred architecture. Its uniform interior space fronted by a powerful facade represented a completely new structural and conceptual approach. Architects Giacomo della Porta and Vignola no longer set classical elements side by side in regular, harmonious order according to a preconceived system of proportions. Instead, visual hierarchies became the rule, and the primary focus of an architect's efforts. Flat surfaces and voluminous forms were rhythmically arranged, giving solid walls and support elements a sense of movement. Baroque buildings were just as energetic in plan as they were in elevation. Both the structure of the walls and their decoration were rendered sculpturally, as if the entire building were a living, breathing work of art. Painting and architectural sculpture were easily, and often spectacularly, integrated into the vision.

Court and church hired renowned artists and architects to bring their ideas to fruition. The extent to which builders and architects were dependent on each other led to heated rivalries. During the seventeenth century, a succession of popes alternately favored first Bernini, and then his rival Borromini. Their lifelong conflict has been interpreted as a struggle between creative geniuses, or simply as a whim encouraged by competing courts. Both are emblematic of the divergent artistic trends of baroque Rome.

This renunciation of long-standing aesthetic norms was given the derogatory name "baroque," which stems from a Portuguese word for pearls of lesser value because of their surface irregularities and lack of symmetry. Today, the term applies to the art and architecture of the entire seventeenth century and most of the eighteenth, as well, although there are considerable variations in style during that period. French baroque architecture, for example, retained more of the classical spirit than Italian baroque, where swelling, swooping, exaggerated forms were more common.

Rococo refers to the period roughly from 1720 to 1770, contemporary with the latest phase of the baroque. It began in France, and spread to Germany, Austria, and Bohemia, where great monastic churches, pilgrimage shrines, and palaces were built in this style.

"Ancient" architecture, based on the forms of ancient Greece and Rome, provided the model for neoclassical architecture. The very name calls forth images of monumental, axial buildings composed of severe, undecorated forms, the very embodiment of the "noble simplicity and quiet grandeur" promoted by antiquarian scholar Johann Joachim Winckelmann. Neoclassical architecture was understood as a reflection of rationalism, a mirror in stone of the reason that would form the foundation for a new social order throughout the Western world.

Above: **Salamanca,** S. Esteban, detail from altar screen, José Benito de Churriguera, 1692–1694.

Left: **Neresheim,** abbey church, dome with fresco by Martin Knoller, 1770–1775.

Opposite: **Rome,** S. Ivo alla Sapienza, Francesco Borromini, begun1643. This university church was built inside a courtyard by Giacomo della Porta. Its facade is an exedra.

Pablo de la Riestra
A Typical Baroque Church Building

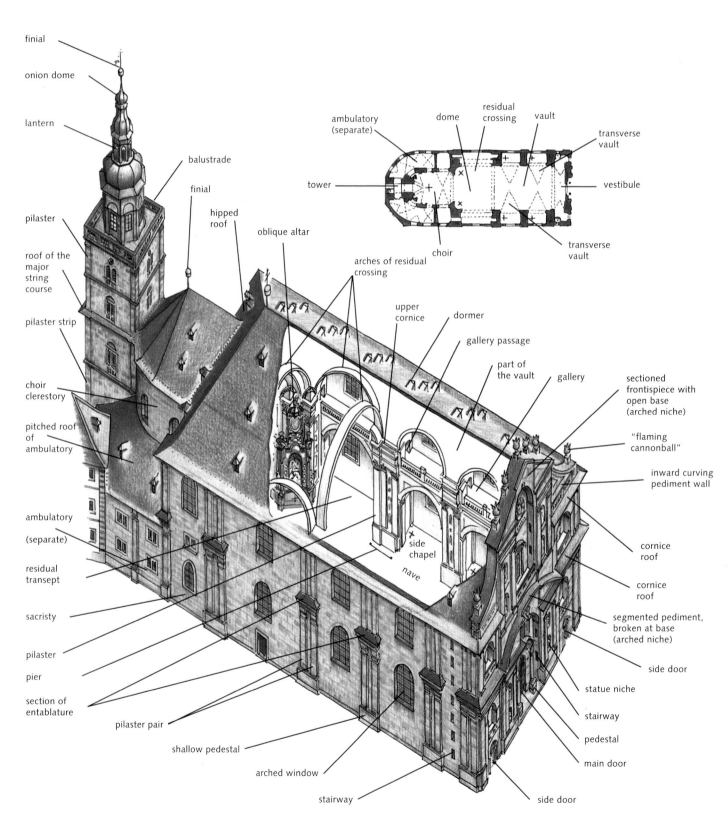

finial

onion dome

lantern

pilaster

roof of the major string course

pilaster strip

choir clerestory

pitched roof of ambulatory

ambulatory (separate)

residual transept

sacristy

pilaster

pier

section of entablature

balustrade

finial

hipped roof

oblique altar

pilaster pair

shallow pedestal

arched window

stairway

ambulatory (separate)

tower

choir

dome

residual crossing

vault

transverse vault

vestibule

transverse vault

arches of residual crossing

upper cornice

dormer

gallery passage

part of the vault

gallery

side chapel

nave

sectioned frontispiece with open base (arched niche)

"flaming cannonball"

inward curving pediment wall

cornice roof

cornice roof

segmented pediment, broken at base (arched niche)

side door

statue niche

stairway

pedestal

main door

side door

Mannerism – Baroque – Rococo
Axonometric drawings with plan, interior, and exterior views

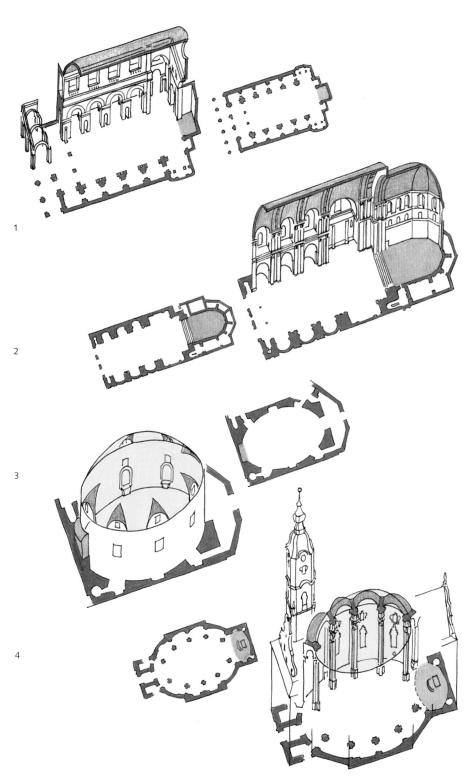

1 Pier church with galleries and residual transept; the chapels are interconnected (Evora, the Jesuit Church of Espiritu Santu, 1567).

2 Pier church with side chapels and residual transept. The gallery bays above the side chapels are interconnected. The barrel vault is somewhat stilted (Munich, Jesuit Church of St Michael).

3 Small oval-plan nave church with altar niche, pendentive vault, and niche-like choir (Madrid, S. Antonio de los Alemanes, 1624–1633).

4 Oval hall church with tower facade and transverse oval choir (Steinhausen, St Peter and St Paul, Dominikus Zimmermann, 1728–1733).

Gianlorenzo Bernini as architect

Gianlorenzo Bernini was born in 1598 Naples, the son of a mason. He arrived in Rome in 1605, where, under papal contract, he created his most enduring sculptural-architectural masterpieces. By the time of his death in 1680, he had only left Rome for one extended period of time, when he went to Paris to advise King Louis XIV on the plans for the Louvre.

Bernini's works went far beyond the artistic norms of his time. His tombs and statues, his baldachin in St Peter's, and his fountain on the Piazza Navona created an illusion of space that opened new perspectives in art. Bernini's architectural career began when Pope Urban VIII commissioned him to renovate S. Bibiana. He was named building master of St Peter's in 1629 (see pp. 180–183) and beginning in 1656 produced the magnificent St Peter's Square.

Left: **Rome,** Il Gesù, 1568–1584, Giacomo Barozzi da Vignola (design and interior), and Giacomo della Porta (facade).

Below: **Rome,** S. Susanna, facade by Carlo Maderno, 1597–1603.

The Early Baroque in Rome

Between the sixteenth and eighteenth centuries, Rome was reinvented by Popes Sixtus V, Paul V, and Urban VIII. They commissioned the great urban axes still integral to the city and funded construction, or reconstruction, of countless churches and palaces.

Il Gesù, the mother church of the Jesuit order, was key to the growth of baroque architecture. The 1568 facade by Giacomo della Porta was a visual statement of the anticlassical sentiments that had already emerged in mannerism. Its interior, by Giacomo da Vignola, was also innovative. He conceived a sacred space completely in line with the precepts of the Tridentine Council, itself an early manifestation of the Counter Reformation. Il Gesù's compact, single-aisle, barrel-vaulted nave with a barely defined transept and shallow side chapels provides even large congregations an unobstructed view of the altar. Il Gesù became the prototypical church for all of Europe, and the New World.

The impact of the facade increasingly became a focus of attention, allotted ever greater importance within the overall design. Architect Carlo Maderno introduced a new dynamic with his groundbreaking facade for S. Susanna. He was also given the task of transforming St Peter's on Vatican Hill from a pure central-plan building to one with a nave and facade. Despite a number of engineering challenges, Maderno's solution to a problem that had stymied many of his predecessors was a magnificent success.

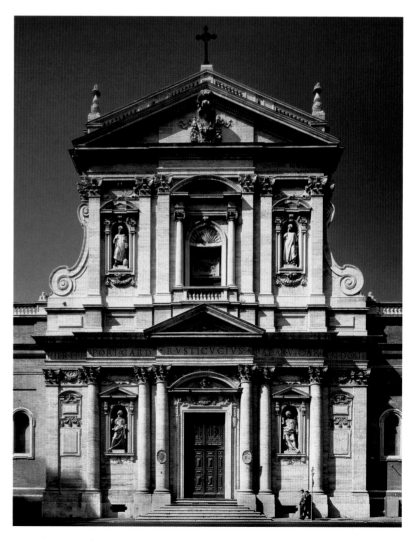

Rome, S. Andrea al Quirinale

Gianlorenzo Bernini worked on S Andrea al Quirinale from 1658 to 1661. The highpoint of this oval-plan building is his theatrical conception of the main altar, which recalls an aedicule. From the pediment over the altar, a statue of the church's patron rises up as if ascending to a golden heaven visible in the brightly illuminated dome above. The figure's gestures correspond to those of the martyr himself as portrayed in the altar painting below. The facade of the church is similarly magnificently coordinated. A baldachin supported by two Ionic columns projects boldly forward, far out in front of the temple-like elevation, while two concave flanking walls invoke an imaginary forecourt.

Below left and right: **Rome,**
S. Andrea al Quirinale, Gianlorenzo
Bernini, 1658–1661, altar niche and
exterior with hemispherical portico.

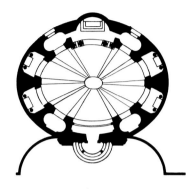

Rome, S. Andrea al Quirinale

Borromini in Rome: S. Andrea delle Fratte

Eccentric misfit, or visionary genius? Enemy of architecture, or its savior? To this day, opinion is sharply divided on the life and work of Francesco Castelli, known as Borromini. He arrived in Rome in his twenties and found work as a mason on the construction of St Peter's. Born in 1599 in Bissone, Borromini came from a long line of masons, and was highly skilled in all the arts of building. His lifelong competition with his rival, Bernini, overshadows his own, very real accomplishments. He died in 1667, by suicide.

Borromini's predilection for fantasy and independence of design is readily visible in his bell tower for the Church of S. Andrea delle Fratte (1653–1656). The pilasters are transformed into cherubim; the volutes surrounding the lantern support a crown of thorns. The artist even manages to wrest an elegant, sinuous profile out of the rough brick drum of the dome.

Rome, S. Agnese

In 1653, Borromini took over as master builder of S. Agnese in Agone. The church is located in a prominent position on the Piazza Navona, where it is part of the Palazzo Pamphili, family seat of Pope Innocent X. The original architect, Girolamo Rainaldi, had worked on the project for just one year before being replaced, and Borromini's term was no less fraught with difficulty. After continuous arguments about the plans, he was relieved of his duties after four years. Carlo Rainaldi, son of the original architect, took over the construction. It was he who succeeded in executing Borromini's magnificent plans for a multi-domed interior fronted by a dramatically detailed facade.

Concave walls and tall attics frame two bell towers, placed well away from one another on either side of the central facade, where they rise into the sky like twin baldachins. Behind this impressive architectural screen, a tall lantern crowns the central dome. This spatially ambitious concept gives S. Agnese a tension-filled, transitional quality. The building has a seemingly ever-changing relationship to the Piazza Navona, which received its present design at this period. The double tower facade with high dome rising behind it would become a prototype of baroque sacred architecture.

Above: **Rome,** S. Andrea delle Fratte, Francesco Borromini, dome and bell tower, 1653–1656.

Opposite: **Rome,** S. Agnese, Francesco Borromini and Carlo Rainaldi, 1652–1657; the facade was completed in 1666.

Rome, S. Maria in Campitelli

Above: **Rome,** S. Maria in Campitelli, Carlo Rainaldi, 1655–1667, interior.

In addition to Bernini and Borromini, Carlo Rainaldi stands as a pivotal figure in the early baroque period in Rome. He designed and constructed the Church of S. Maria in Campitelli under contract to Pope Alexander VII. After working out an oval plan, he settled on a more ambitious design based on the intersection of two Greek crosses. The interior is more audacious still. Freestanding columns draw the eye to a dramatically designed altar space.

Pietro da Cortona

For Pietro da Cortona, born Pietro Berrettini in Tuscany in 1597, architecture was a hobby, a way of passing the time. He completed very few buildings, but these soon became known as the very epitome of baroque style.

This exceptionally talented painter, draftsman, stage designer, and principle of Rome's premier art academy (Accademia di S. Luca) took over the renovation of his institute's church in 1635. After workmen found the remains of S. Martina during construction, the decision was made to build a magnificent new church instead. Cortona designed a straightforward centrally planned building in the form of a Greek cross, but gave it an extraordinary lively, sculptural interior. Its walls are a play of columns and piers, with white and grey reliefs articulating the intervening spaces, filling the curve of the vault. The facade is in motion, with atypical convex walls bulging forward between double pilasters. The impression is that

Left and below: **Rome,**
SS Luca e Martina, Pietro da Cortona, 1635–1660, interior and facade.

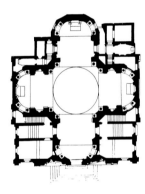

Rome, SS. Luca e Martina

the spatial volume of the interior is expanding, pressing outward against the front of the church from inside.

Cortona's design for the facade of S. Maria della Pace (1656–1657) is another milestone in Roman baroque. The ground floor is a hemispherical portico, with concave side wings picking up and transferring its movement across the front of the building.

His final masterpiece was the classically elegant dome of S. Carlo al Corso (begun in 1668). Its silhouette still towers over Rome today.

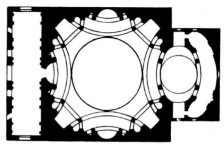

Turin, S. Lorenzo

Left: **Turin,** S. Lorenzo, Guarino
Guarini, 1668–1687, view of the
dome.

Turin and the Vicinity

Outside of Rome, Turin was one of the few urban
centers that contributed to the development of
baroque architecture. Three of the most important
architects of the late baroque period—Guarino
Guarini, Filippo Juvarra, and Bernardo Vittone—
worked out of the city's princely residences, and for
other patrons nearby.

Before taking up architecture, Guarino Guarini was a Theatine monk, philosopher, and mathematician from Modena. His dynamic direction of
interior and exterior space defines him as a successor of Borromini. In 1668–1687, he worked on
Turin's S. Lorenzo, a centrally planned church with
a dome supported by freestanding arches. The
colorfully banded ribs of the dome may be an influence from Moorish architecture.

The gifted architect and draftsman Filippo
Juvarra began his career in service to Piedmontese
ruler Vittorio Amedeos II. His earliest work in
Turin is probably his best: the votive church La
Superga, which served as a mausoleum for members of the Savoy dynasty. Its dome is set on an
exceptionally tall drum. Its facade, designed to be
visible from far away, emphasizes the strong re-
cession of the monastic buildings behind. In La
Superga, Juvarra captured the essential ideas of the
Roman high baroque and placed them in an
entirely new setting: a rural landscape.

Left: **Turin,** La Superga,
Filippo Juvarra, 1717–1731.

Bra, S. Chiara

Bernardo Vittone (1705–1770) stood in the shadow of his more famous colleagues, Guarini and Juvarra. The artistic quality of his work has only recently been recognized.

Vittone initially studied in Rome, but spent nearly his entire professional career in the Piedmont region designing exceptional, picturesque churches. He was also interested in theory, publishing Guarini's treatise *Architettura Civile* after the latter's death.

S. Chiara in Bra (1742) is a good example of his exquisitely artistry. A centrally planned building, like most of his churches, S. Chiara unites Guarini's precisely calculated dome structures with Juvarra's lavish approach to dramatically designed interiors.

Above: **Bra,** S. Chiara, Bernardo Vittone, 1742, interior of the dome.

Classicizing "Temples" in Italy

A renewed encounter with ancient architecture led to a revival of classicism. In contrast to the Renaissance, scholars were now looking not only to Roman ruins, but also to ancient Greece, home of the Greek temple, as the preferred source for architectural inspiration. There was considerable dispute in the years around 1750 as to the supremacy of one ancient model over the other, which led to a new, eclectic approach combining elements of both.

By the early nineteenth century, the Roman Pantheon was popularly considered the ideal. The relationship between the temple facade and round building corresponded to the prevailing interest in basic forms and rationalism. At the same time, the Pantheon was an expressly urban building, easily integrated into a theatrically conceived streetscape or plaza. The Foro Murat in Naples, begun by Napoleon in 1809, is a good example. A Pantheon-styled church sits in the center of a hemispherical colonnade. The architect and mason Canova also "fell for" the prototype, and contributed a building of surpassing beauty modeled on the Pantheon to his home city of Possagno.

Opposite and above: **Possagno,** Tempio Canoviano, Antonio Canova and Giovanni Antonio Selva (?), 1819–1833.

Below: **Naples,** Foro Murat (later Foro Ferdinandeo), Leopoldo Laperuta, begun 1809. S. Francesco di Paola (1836) by Pietro Bianchi stands in the center.

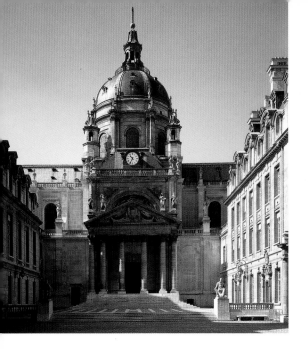

Above: **Paris,** Church of the Sorbonne, Jacques Lemercier, begun 1626, courtyard facade.

It was up to Jules Hardouin-Mansart to create the quintessential French baroque church: Les Invalides (1706), also known as the "Church of the Dome" after its most prominent feature. Actually a central-plan building connected to the nave of an older hospital church, Hardouin-Mansart's masterpiece is a superb synthesis of two disparate elements: the block-like, rectilinear prism of the lower building and a domineering, high-drummed dome that recalls St. Peter's in Rome.

The transition to neoclassicism is further defined by the Royal Chapel of Versailles Palace, begun by Hardouin-Mansart and completed by Robert de Cotte. The gallery church unites ancient, medieval, and baroque elements. French kings were consecrated here, a role once held by the Sainte-Chapelle.

Opposite: **Versailles,** Royal Chapel, Jules Hardouin-Mansart and Robert de Cotte, 1689–1710, interior.

Below: **Paris,** Les Invalides, Liberal Bruant and Jules Hardouin-Mansart, 1677–1706.

Baroque Churches in and near Paris

In contrast to its thriving, innovative chateau architecture, French churches were slow to adopt new styles. When they did, innovation took the form of monumental domed buildings that majestically define the Paris cityscape.

The university church at the Sorbonne was a milestone in the development of the French baroque. The domed central-plan building, with its prominent articulated west facade, is reminiscent of Roman models. Other influences come into play in the courtyard elevation, where picturesque, theatrical motifs dominate the arrangement of temple front, triumphal arch, hipped roof, and high-drummed dome. The church combines both classical and baroque ideas in one uniquely spectacular building.

The votive church commissioned on the occasion of the birth of the heir to the throne is another dramatic domed building. Val-de-Grâce was begun in 1645 by François Mansart, continued by Lemercier, and completed by Pierre Le Muet and Gabriel Le Duc. Here as well, Roman architecture provides the template; Mansart, who designed the church from the floor plan to roof beams, gave it a new, enhanced monumentality.

Paris, Panthéon (Ste-Geneviève)

By the middle of the eighteenth century, a number of influential voices were calling for a rethinking of baroque sacred architecture. The ideal now was a return to the straightforward, clean lines of antiquity. The new abbey and pilgrimage church of Ste-Geneviève in Paris offered a prime opportunity to put these classical concepts into practice, albeit in a much modified form.

Jacques-Germain Soufflot was determined to create a building on the Greek cross plan that was monumental, but at the same time, surpassingly elegant. He decided on a Corinthian temple front, with the towering dome of the crossing rising behind it. With St Paul's in London as his model, he ringed the drum of the dome with slender columns. His technical mastery is evident in the illumination of the interior. With the help of iron beams and relieving arches, Soufflot was able to insert enormous windows in all the walls. Unfortunately, when the building was transformed into France's Panthéon des Grands Hommes (Pantheon of Great Men), most of those windows were partially or entirely filled in. In the process, the original atmosphere, full of light and space, has been to a large extent lost.

Paris, Church of the Madeleine

In 1806, Napoleon commissioned a secular church, a "temple of glory" in honor of his Grande Armée. Pierre-Alexandre Vignon won the contest for the

Opposite and left: **Paris**, La Madeleine, Pierre-Alexandre Vignon, 1807–1842.

Above: **Paris,** Panthéon, formerly Ste-Geneviève, Jacques-Germain Soufflot, 1757–1790.

design, taking the word "temple" very literally indeed. Soon, a Corinthian peripteros, a temple surrounded on all sides by columns, rose at the end of the rue Royale. With the restoration of the monarchy and crowning of Louis XVIII, the Église de la Madeleine was consecrated as a royal church. The building itself, however, was only completed in 1842. The interior, originally designed to comply with "pagan" models, was given a new look with more appropriately Christian decor plastered onto the bare walls. The church's sequence of three rooms was meant to invoke the architecture of a Roman bath; marble incrustation is a reference to the original Pantheon in Rome.

Baroque Facades in Spain

Spanish architecture in the baroque period was long under the influence of the Spanish court, which favored the severe classicism of buildings like the monastery of El Escorial. It was the mid-seventeenth century before certain regions of Spain were able to step out from under the shadow of the crown. It is their architecture that marks the true beginning of the Spanish baroque.

In Jerez, the abbey church of the Carthusian monastery Nuestra Señora de la Defensión is a good example of a style devoted to dissolution of the walls behind a curtain of evocative decoration. Developed in Andalusia, its technical and artistic masters were the eighteenth-century architects Francisco de Hurtados and the brothers Churriguera.

During the seventeenth century, the northwestern province of Galacia was home to a regional, independent, highly creative approach to baroque architecture. The 1649 Cathedral of Santiago de Compostela, already an impressive building, was enhanced during the eighteenth century by the addition of a new facade. The task facing its architects was not without its challenges. The new facade had to conceal, but also protect and showcase, a preexisting Romanesque portal called the Portico de la Gloria. This meant that the new facade could not be solid; it had to let in light. The final condition was that the earlier baroque staircase be integrated into the total design. Architect Fernando Casas y Novoa solved the problem with remarkable skill. He concealed the Romanesque portal behind a curtain wall flanked by two towers, with the central part of the facade opened up by enormous windows. The technical achievement alone was considerable, the artistic even more so. His lively use of vertical elements, including columns on top of columns, staggered towers, and telescoping broken-topped gables, draws the eye in all directions. The intricate decoration covering the central wall reminded contemporaries of fine metalwork. This may be why it is called *la fachada del obradoiro* (goldwork facade).

The Cathedral of Murcia is an example of the architectural achievements of the Levantine region. Its spatially complex ordering of architectural elements to create multiple planes makes its facade both monumental and delicate.

Above: **Jerez de la Frontera,** Carthusian Abbey Church Nuestra Señora de la Defensión, 1667, facade.

Left: **Murcia,** cathedral, Jaime Bort, 1742–1754, facade.

Opposite: **Santiago de Compostela,** facade (*fachada del obradoiro*), Fernando Casas y Novoa, 1738.

Retables and Tabernacles

Retables and tabernacles took on monumental proportions during the Spanish baroque, often becoming the showpiece of a church interior. Behind the main altar in Toledo Cathedral, Narciso Tomé's El Transparente, an enormous monstrance several stories tall, is an intoxicating *gesamtkunstwerk*. Its name—"the transparent one"—comes from the deliberately engineered effect of sunlight striking the retable through a slit in the dome. The angels and saints appear to float in light, giving us a view through the veil of the material world into heaven itself.

The retable at S. Esteban in Salamanca is the founding example of the Churrigueresque style, named after the family of architects who popularized it over several generations. It makes ample use of Solomonic (twisted) columns, dramatic spatial arrangements, and rich, even florid, decoration of every available surface.

Emblematic of the period is the excessive decoration of the interiors of two late baroque Carthusian abbey churches by Francisco de Hurtado Izquierdo. He took classical elements and distorted them prismatically, breaking them down and recombining them into a multitude of complex decorative formulas. His influence extended from Andalusia to the colonial baroque architecture of the New World.

Opposite: **Granada,** Carthusian
abbey church, Francisco de Hurtado
Izquierdo, 1702–1720.

Above: **Toledo,** cathedral,
El Transparente, Narciso
Tomé, 1721–1732.

Right: **Salamanca,** S.
Esteban, retable, José Benito
de Churriguera, 1692–1694.

Baroque Churches in Portugal

Portuguese baroque architecture is strongly oriented toward late mannerist models, as is evident in the facade of Igreja dos Grilos in the city of Porto. Spread by treatises published throughout Europe, the style was widespread in Portugal and Spain by the end of the seventeenth century. Portugal was experiencing an unprecedented boom at the time, sparked by the discovery of gold and diamonds in the colony of Brazil. This had an immediate effect on the country's architecture. King João V believed he could turn Lisbon into a second Rome.

In Porto, near the royal court, a local architectural style began to develop based on the work of Siena architect Nicola Nasoni. Both Portuguese and Brazilian sacred architecture would favor the concept of a Sacro Monte, or sacred mount, where the church is set on a hill ascended by a long staircase representing the stations of the cross. Visitors climbing the staircase thereby shared in the experience of Christ's Passion. In the sanctuary of Bom Jesus do Monte near Braga, pagan allegorical figures are interspersed with Christian iconography.

Opposite: **Braga,** Bom Jesus do Monte, 1784–1811, stations of the cross and facade of the church.

Below left: **Porto,** Igreja dos Grilos, facade, Baltasar Alvares, 1622.

Below right: **Porto,** Torre des Clérigos, Nicola Nasoni, 1757–1763.

Middle and South America

The Catholic church played a decisive role in Spanish and Portuguese colonial history. With religion providing a justification for the conquest of the extensive mineral-rich territories of the New World, there was a correspondingly greater need to impress the nonbelievers that the church hoped to convert. Architecture and its sublime visual rhetoric would be an important part of this mission.

The first colonization phase focused on securing strategic and administrative control of the newly conquered territories. The Viceroyalty of Spain was founded in 1535, encompassing the Caribbean and Central America. The Viceroyalty of Peru followed in 1542; it would eventually expand to include what are today Argentina, Chile, and Uruguay. Meanwhile, the Portuguese ruled in Brazil, which is by far the largest country in South America.

Between the sixteenth and eighteenth centuries, the New World colonial powers built a great many cathedrals, congregational churches, missions, and pilgrimage sites. Secular archi-

Left: **Havana, Cuba**, cathedral facade, begun 1742.

Below: **Mexico City**, cathedral, begun 1573.

Above: **Guadalajara, Mexico**,
cathedral, from 1542.

tecture was relegated to the background. The most important cathedrals were located in diocesan administrative centers such as La Antigua, Guatemala; Havana, Cuba; Mexico City, Puebla, Mexico; Quito, Ecuador; Cuzco and Lima in Peru; and La Paz, Bolivia. Natural disasters—earthquakes, fires, and floods—have taken their toll, and very few of these buildings survive in their original, unadulterated style. The majority have been restored and renovated many times over.

The earliest stylistic influences were European, primarily Spanish, specifically the mannerist architecture popular in Andalusia. Over the course of the seventeenth and eighteenth centuries, however, a regional Latin American design vocabulary began to emerge. In Mexico and the Andes states, the central element of the facade became an opulently decorated triumphal arch. While the architectural philosophy of Latin American sacred buildings was still derived from mannerist treatises, the decorative program was expanded to include native motifs based on plants and animals familiar to the indigenous population. Richly embellished interiors were so opulently wrought with gold, intricately carved wood, elaborate stucco moldings, and brightly colored tile that the room itself recedes from view. In a

conscious reference to Early Christian models, Mexican churches are characterized by quatrefoil atria, forecourts where heathens could receive instruction. Similarly geared toward practical concerns are the open chapels, a reaction to the nature-oriented lives of the natives.

Mexico City Cathedral is one of the largest in Latin America. Construction began in 1573 according to plans by Claudio de Arciniega, a Spanish architect, who took Seville Cathedral in Andalusia as his model. This monumental five-aisled hall church replaced an older, more modest structure on the same site, itself erected over the ruins of an Aztec temple. The cathedral complex was completed only in 1813. The lengthy period of construction is readily evident in the variety of architectural styles in its facade and porticos.

The foundation stone of Guadalajara Cathedral was laid shortly after the founding of the city in 1542. It, too, was frequently rebuilt and renovated, with its dominant style alternating between classicism and baroque. The facade, gold-tiled tower, and massive dome are part of a nineteenth-century reconstruction carried out after part of the church was destroyed by an earthquake.

The old city of Havana around the Plaza de Armas is dominated by the curvaceous, late baroque facade of the city's cathedral. Begun in 1742 and completed in 1777, it is thought to be the work of the Andalusian architect Pedro de Medina.

Argentina and Brazil

Above left: **Santa Fe (Argentina)**, S. Francisco, interior with wooden ceiling that imitates a dome, ca. 1680.

Above right: **Córdoba (Argentina)**, cathedral, begun 1680.

In 1542, the Spanish-dominated parts of South America were united under the Viceroyalty of Peru. Bourbon administrative reforms led to the formation of the Viceroyalty of Rio de la Plata in 1776, which included what are today the countries of Argentina, Paraguay, and Uruguay. The colonization of these regions was exceedingly arduous, and plagued by setbacks. The first successful Spanish settlements were clustered along the eastern slopes of the Andes. Even there, the city of Buenos Aires, founded in 1536, had to be abandoned a few years later. It was eventually resettled in 1580.

Córdoba, today the second largest city in Argentina, was founded in 1573, and became the site of a Jesuit university in 1613. The Church of Nuestra Señora de la Asunción was begun in 1680, and elevated to cathedral status in 1699. Its facade takes the form of a triumphal arch flanked by two later towers (1804). The exquisite baroque dome is a late-seventeenth-century addition by Seville architect Fray Vicente Muñoz. The cathedral is both a symbol of Córdoba and a major monument of Argentinean colonial architecture. Another important work of Argentinean colonial art is the vault of the Franciscan church in Santa Fe, a northeastern provincial capital. The ceiling is a masterpiece of the Mudéjar style, a blend of Moorish and Spanish elements

popular during the sixteenth century in Spain, after which it was exported to the colonies.

Portuguese colonization was at first limited to the eastern coast of the continent. The most important city, and seat of the Governor General until 1763, was São Salvador de Bahia. It was said that it had "more churches than there are days in the year." Most of its sacred architecture followed Portuguese models, such as the nave churches common in Lisbon and Coimbras. These usually had a two-tower facade, or were mannerist in the style promoted by theoretician Sebastiano Serlio. Only São Francisco da Ordem Terceira has elaborate facade decoration typical of the Spanish-influenced Andes states. By the late eighteenth century, Brazil was developing its own elegant version of late baroque architecture, most prominently in the gold- and diamond-rich region of Minas Gerais. The central-plan interiors are entered through convex-concave facades with towers set behind them. The sheer plasticity of forms throughout the buildings is unique in Latin America. The architect, Aleijadinho (Antônio Francisco Lisboa), is one of the few early colonial architects whose life is well documented. He was of mixed heritage and, judging by his

Left: **Ouro Preto, Brazil**,
São Francisco de Assis, Aleijadinho
(Antônio Francisco Lisboa), 1765–1775.

Above: **Rio de Janeiro**, Monastery
of São Bento, interior, begun 1617,
renovations and decoration from 1668.

name (*aleijado* = crippled), was also physically disabled. His life remains a subject of study.

The sumptuous interiors of Brazilian baroque churches are without compare. Gilded, intricately carved wood paneling (*talha dourada*) covers every surface of the walls, support elements, and ceilings, blurring the boundaries between structure, sculpture, and ornament. High-relief figures of saints, allegorical personifications, foliage, and geometric motifs merge to form a glorious whole. One of the most beautiful is the Benedictine church of the São Bento Monastery in Rio de Janeiro. Its simple, sober, twin-towered facade opens into a space that could hardly be more sumptuous. The entire interior seems to have been dipped in gold, and elaborate carvings cover the walls, arches, and altars. The church was begun in 1617 from plans by Francisco de Frias de Mesquita. It was only completed near the end of that century. The unique interior decor was the work of Frei Domingos da Conceição and his studio. There are a few similarly exuberant churches in São Salvador de Bahia, of which the Franciscan church in the colonial neighborhood of Terreiro de Jesus is the best known. Its opulent decor was executed from 1738 to 1740.

Above: **Löwen,** St Michael, Willem Hesius and others, 1550–1666, facade.

Right top and bottom: **Brussels,** St Johann Baptist, Lucas Fayd'herbe, 1657–1677, facade and interior.

Belgium

In the mid-sixteenth century, what is today the country of Belgium developed its own rich decorative style while still under the control of Spanish rulers. Traces of mannerism survive in the use of scrollwork and cartouche borders, while elements of the late Gothic aare continued in the domes.

London, St. Paul's Cathedral

In September 1666, the Great Fire of London reduced thirteen thousand houses, St Paul's Cathedral, and eighty-seven city churches to soot and ashes. King George II commissioned Christopher Wren and his colleagues Roger Pratt and Hugh May to come up with a new, more modern city plan. In the end, Wren's plan was considered unworkable, but the rebuilding of St Paul's Cathedral, along with fifty-one parish churches, was completed largely according to his design.

The ongoing rivalry between (Anglican) St Paul's in London and (Catholic) St Peter's in Rome informed Wren's master plan. His Great Model, presented to the king in 1673, is reminiscent of Michelangelo's domed central plan. After many revisions, a more traditional long-nave church was built, with a gigantic crossing dome rising 365 feet (111 m) into the air. The main facade is a visually unified, two-story, Louvre-influenced, columned portico flanked by two towers. Clever combinations of disparate elements continue in the interior, where the domed space and transept are willfully fitted into the more traditionally proportioned long nave and choir. Academic classicism dominates the interior space.

Despite numerous conceptual discontinuities, many of which can be traced back to the extended period of construction (1675–1711), St Paul's Cathedral, and especially its dome, became one of the most emulated Anglican sacred buildings in the world. The appeal of a plan that began by reproducing an important Roman Catholic church is all the more surprising considering that, just a few years earlier, the adoption of Catholic elements in Protestant architecture had been more or less officially banned.

Right top and bottom: **London,** St Paul's Cathedral, Sir Christopher Wren, 1675–1711, interior and exterior views.

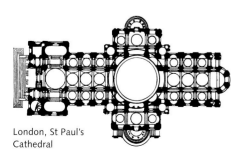

London, St Paul's Cathedral

Stockholm, Riddarholmen Church Mausoleum

Scandinavia made a significant contribution to the architecture of the seventeenth and eighteenth centuries. Its unique stylistic contribution is a material-based aesthetic, specifically decorative brickwork, sculpted sandstone decoration, and copper-plated roofs. The models for Scandinavian architecture in general (not merely its Protestant sacred buildings) were usually found in the Netherlands. But it was the 1639 elevation of a French architect, Simon de la Vallée (d. 1642) to the position of Royal Architect that was the deciding factor in the success of baroque classicism in Sweden. His son, Jean de la Vallée, and his son's successors, Nicodemus Tessin the Older, and Nicodemus Tessin the Younger, brought Swedish baroque architecture the international acclaim it so richly deserved.

The elegant mausoleum of Charles VIII flanks the northern side of the Gothic Riddarholmen Church in Stockholm. Many Swedish kings were laid to rest in this former Franciscan monastery church. The mausoleum has a central, Greek cross plan, and Tuscan columns. It was begun in 1675 by Nicodemus Tessin the Older, but was only completed in the mid-seventeenth century under the supervision of architect Carl Hårleman. The elegant formal relationship between the baroque and classical elements reflects influences absorbed by Tessin during his extensive travels through central, western, and southern Europe.

Left: **Stockholm,** Riddarholmen Church, mausoleum of Charles VIII, Nicodemus Tessin the Older, 1675–1761.

Above and opposite: **Breslau (Wrocław, Poland)**, Elector's Chapel, Johann Bernhard Fischer von Erlach, 1716–1724, interior; view from the east of the Elizabeth, Lady, and Elector Chapels, 14th-18th centuries.

Breslau (Wrocław) Cathedral, Poland

Breslau's medieval cathedral received two ornate chapels during the baroque period, erected on either side of the Gothic Lady Chapel on the eastern side of the building. The southern chapel (left in the picture) is dedicated to St Elizabeth. It was completed between 1680 and 1700 by Giacomo Scanzi and his studio. The northern chapel (right in the picture) was built after 1716 following a plan by the exceptionally talented Viennese architect Johann Bernhard Fischer von Erlach. It houses what is known as the Elector's Chapel, the final resting place of the Grand Master of the German Knights, Franz Ludwig zu Pfalz-Neuberg. The bishops of Breslau are also interred there. Rectilinear in plan, the interior space is crowned by a massive dome set atop a drum pierced with windows. The focus of the room is a rounded altar niche displaying a gilded replica of the Ark of the Covenant.

Franz Ludwig was the nephew of Hapsburg Emperor Leopold I, and thus in close contact with the Viennese court and the many artists and architects serving there. In addition to Austrian and Italian architects, the Dutchman Tylman van Gameren played an important role in the development of baroque architecture in Poland. After the House of Wettin assumed the Polish crown in 1607, architects from Saxony arrived in Warsaw, among them Matthäus Daniel Pöppelmann and Zacharias Longelune.

Above: **Salzburg,** cathedral, Santino Solari, begun 1614, view to the east with crossing dome.

Opposite: **Munich,** St Michael, 1583–1597, interior.

Munich, St Michael

St Michael in Munich, the masterpiece of an unknown architect, is one of the first important buildings to emerge from the German baroque period. Its design unites the standard design of Il Gesù in Rome with the local pier church. The massive, hall-like nave is spanned by a 65-foot (20-m) wide barrel vault—the second largest ever built—supported on the transverse walls and vaults of the side chapels. The abundant light combined with the white decoration lends the interior the festive glow of a ballroom.

Salzburg Cathedral

The 1614 rebuilding of Salzburg Cathedral was supervised by northern Italian architect Santino Solari. The plan of the cathedral, however, suggests very different influences. It combines a domed church with a triconch plan that recalls Romanesque examples. Here as well, the focus is on the decoration of the interior spaces, where lavish, exuberant motifs emphasize the underlying architectural structure. This kind of interior would reach the heights of artistic expression in the eighteenth century.

Johann Bernhard Fischer von Erlach

Roman drama unites with pictorial decor in the work of Vienna architect Johann Bernhard Fischer von Erlach. Fischer's early buildings are clearly influenced by Bernini and Borromini, whose works he had studied in Rome. His three Salzburg churches—Dreifaltigkeitskirche (Holy Trinity), the collegiate church, and the Ursuline convent church—are assemblies of sharply defined cubic elements dynamically projecting into space. Like their Roman predecessors, they are well integrated into their urban context. In fact, it was the express desire of their patron, Archbishop Johann Ernst Baron Thun, that Salzburg be transformed into "the Rome of

the North." With his Karlskirche in Vienna, Fischer created the emblematic building of Hapsburg Austria. His concept united votive church—it was built in the wake of the plague of 1713—with masterful visual statement. A dome set on a high drum dominates the long oval of the interior, which is entered through a classical portico set between two classicizing triumphal columns, themselves flanked by two

Below: **Vienna,** Karlskirche (Church of St Charles Borromeo), Johann Bernhard Fischer von Erlach, 1716–1737, view into the dome.

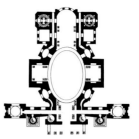

Vienna, Karlskirche

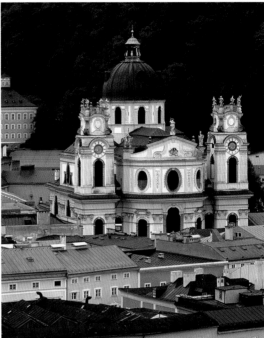

squat towers. The facade is a truly magnificent integration of multiple levels of architectural iconography that both proclaim the political dimension of the Hapsburg Empire and, in response to the imperial aspirations of the Spanish court, celebrate its ancient roots.

Top right: **Salzburg,** Collegiate Church, Johann Bernhard Fischer von Erlach, 1694–1703.

Bottom right: **Salzburg,** Dreifaltigkeitskirche (Holy Trinity Church), Johann Bernhard Fischer von Erlach, 1694–1703.

Melk Abbey (Austria)

The prelates of the great baroque abbeys were on par with secular princes when it came to commissioning great buildings. Melk Abbey, on the Danube River in Austria, is a superb example of their worldly and spiritual power. Benedictine abbot Berthold Dietmayer and his architects worked together to create a compelling *gesamtkunstwerk*. Jakob Prandtauer produced the plans around 1701, calling for a twin-towered facade looming over the rocky promontory in the Danube Valley. Its terrace provides a stunning view of the surrounding landscape, picturesquely framed by architectural elements. The abbey is 787 ft (240 m) long, making it visible from very far away. The exhilarating interior of the church is painted with frescoes by Johann Michael Rottmayr showing episodes from the life of St Benedict, founder of the order.

The Dientzenhofer Family of Architects

The Dientzenhofer family produced a number of great architects. Working primarily from Italian models, the Dientzenhofers developed their own, unmistakable style that gave international standing to baroque buildings from Bamberg to Prague.

George Dientzenhofer was the eldest of the clan. In 1682, he moved to the small town of Waldsassen, Germany, and built, without pay, the pilgrimage chapel. The chapel is the epitome of architectural symbolism. The three-sided plan itself is a direct reference to the Holy Trinity.

Johann Dientzenhofer traveled to Bamberg, where he came in contact with the powerful elector Lothar Franz von Schönborn. His Fulda Cathedral, constructed between 1704 and 1713, is considered one of the greatest German churches in the tradition of Il Gesù in Rome.

In the city of Banz, Johann Dientzenhofer's Bohemian heritage, along with the influence of Guarini, come across more strongly. The abbey church high above the harbor on the Main River is a virtuoso play on the dynamics of space. The window and chapel bays of the walls curve in opposition to the arc of the ceiling vaults, giving the interior space a subtle sense of constant motion, a gentle rocking back and forth. The next generation was led by Kilian Ignaz, son of Christoph Dientzenhofer. His late churches are among the most beautiful examples of Bohemian rococo.

Below left: **Kappel near Waldsassen,** pilgrimage chapel, Georg Dientzenhofer, 1685–1689.

Below right: **Banz,** Benedictine abbey church, Johann Dientzenhofer, 1710–1719, interior.

The Vorarlberger School of Architecture and Switzerland

The Vorarlberger school had its strongest influence on the sacred architecture of southwest Germany. Masters of this style built pier churches with chapel niches and galleries. Structural elements were emphasized by elaborate interior decor executed in gleaming white stucco.

The abbey church in Weingarten, lying at the heart of a large monastic complex, is the work of Caspar Moosbrugger in conjunction with Donato Giuseppe Frisoni. Completed between 1715 and 1723, it displays the Vorarlberger school's typical facade consisting of towers on either side of a convex central element, as Fischer von Erlach had done in Salzburg. The bold lines defining the interior space are enhanced by white Wessobruner stucco. Illusionistic ceiling frescoes by Cosmas Damian Asam extend the architectural elements into a clear blue sky.

Swiss baroque architecture was not blind to the Vorarlberger school. The Jesuit Church in Solthurn served as impetus for the spread of Vorarlberger baroque throughout Switzerland. At the same time, variations on the basic pier church could be seen in the abbey church in Einsiedeln. Architect Caspar Moosbrugger devised a complex series of spatial transitions that take into account a variety of different liturgical requirements. A swelling twin-towered facade leads to an octagonal chapel housing a miraculous image. This leads to a transept-like space for the preaching of sermons, followed by a light-filled domed area adorned with Cosmas Damian Asam's monumental frescoes of the birth of Christ. A perspectively illusionistic choir rail separates the public area from the monk's choir, itself a modified version of an older, pre-existing nave.

Above and right: **Weingarten, Germany**, abbey church, Casper Moosbrugger, 1715–1723, exterior and interior views.

Left: **Solothurn, Switzerland**, Jesuit church, Heinrich Mayer, 1680–1689, interior.

Above: **Einsiedeln, Switzerland**, Benedictine abbey church, Hans Georg Kuen, Caspar Moosbrugger, and others, new plan after 1691, construction begun 1719, interior.

Steinhausen, St Peter and St Paul

Rococo churches in the southern German regions of Bavaria and Swabia are among the highpoints of the style. The bright interiors, subtle play of color, and seamless melding of architecture and decor bewitch the senses.

White dominates the interior of the pilgrimage church in Steinhausen, erected in 1727 on the site of an older building. Architect Dominikus Zimmermann's plan is in the form of an elongated ellipse, with the central space delineated to great effect by ten freestanding piers supporting the nave vault. The surface is painted with an illusionistic fresco by Johann Baptist Zimmerman, the architect's brother. The visitor is presented with a vision of paradise unfolding above the soaring piers. A group of saints and allegorical figures surround a central image of the Assumption of the Virgin. The fresco borders vary between the structural and the illusionistic, blurring the distinction between real and illusionistic space, architecture, and nature. The play on the senses is enhanced by delicate floral friezes and stucco animals surprisingly peeking out here and there from walls, moldings, and cornices.

Opposite: **Steinhausen,** St Peter and St Paul, Dominikus Zimmermann, begun 1727, with ceiling fresco by Johann Baptist Zimmerman, 1733.

Right and below: **Birnau,** Church of Our Lady, Peter Thumb (architect), Johann Anton Feuchtmayer (stucco), and Gottfried Bernhard Göz (frescoes), 1745–1751.

Birnau, Unsere Liebe Frau (Church of Our Lady)

The pinnacle of Swabian architecture and decorative art can be found in Birnau, on the shores of Lake Constance. In his 1745 design for the pilgrimage church, architect Peter Thumb, working with sculptor Joseph Anton Feuchtmeyer, created a successful *gesamtkunstwerk* (artistic fusion) in the region's characteristically extravagant decorative style.

Inside, walls are barely discernible behind the lavish interplay of pilasters, galleries, transverse arches, and vaults. The earthly realm melds with the heavenly almost unseen by means of seamless integration of real and illusory architectural elements. The interior's delicate beige color scheme contributes as much to an elegant atmosphere as the delicately molded stucco adorning nearly every surface.

Opposite and below: **Vierzehn-heiligen,** pilgrimage church, Balthasar Neumann, 1743–1772. Facade and interior, with altar shrine.

Above: **Neresheim,** Benedictine abbey church, Balthasar Neumann, begun 1745, interior.

The Churches of Balthasar Neumann

The churches built by the multitalented architect and engineer Balthasar Neumann are both a feast for the senses and a triumph of the art of building.

The Pilgrimage Church of Vierzehnheiligen (Fourteen Saints), near Bamberg, Germany, came into being as part of an emergency solution to an unexpected problem after Neumann stepped in to correct potentially catastrophic mistakes made by his building supervisor, Gottfried Heinrich Krohne. Onto the foundation walls already in place, Neumann imposed a new plan based on circles and ellipses. The central space, accentuated by a ring of piers, contains a scenographic altar with images of the fourteen saints, called upon in times of need, arrayed around it.

If Vierzehnheiligen is a feast for the senses, Neumann's Benedictine abbey church in Neresheim is a feast for the intellect. The cool, white abbey church with its slender, freestanding double columns is both a constructive and aesthetic masterpiece. The building remained without a roof for many years after Neumann's death because the monks wouldn't trust the construction of the stone dome to any other architect. Ultimately, Neumann's design was recreated in wood.

Dresden, Frauenkirche (Church of Our Lady)

The silhouette of the Frauenkirche's towering bell-shaped dome is a symbol of the city of Dresden. The baroque central-plan building with its galleries and tiny rooms was the congregation church of the city's Protestant community following its construction in 1726, and consecration while still incomplete in 1734. The plans for the church were the work of municipal architect George Bähr. On February 15, 1945, the building collapsed in a heap of burning rubble during the Dresden bombing. The decision to rebuild was made in 1990, and in 2005 the Frauenkirche was finally reconsecrated. The reconstruction of the church, for the most part true to the original plans, was funded by public grants and international donations.

Hamburg, St Michael

Next to Our Lady in Dresden, St Michael in Hamburg is the most important Protestant sacred building of the German baroque. Destroyed several times by fire, it underwent numerous reconstructions, including significant alterations, the last of which were carried out in 1907–1912 and after the church was damaged by bombs during World War II. The original baroque building was the work of Johann Leonard Prey and Georg Sonnin between 1751 and 1762. The plan is cruciform, with four massive piers demarking the central space devoted to the preaching of sermons. Elegant curved galleries surround it, overlooking the altar space. The "Michael" tower stands west of the church. Its temple-like crown is a Hamburg landmark.

Above and opposite: **Dresden,** Frauenkirche (Church of Our Lady), George Bähr, begun 1726, reconstructed 1990–2005 following near complete destruction during World War II.

Right: **Hamburg,** St Michael, Johann Leonhard Prey and Georg Sonnin, 1751–1762, interior.

HISTORICISM AND MODERNISM

The Age of Enlightenment brought with it the conviction that there was a God-given order to the world, irrespective of one's spiritual beliefs. This upheaval greatly affected religious institutions, which were in danger of losing their followers to an increased interest in the temporal world. Naturally, sacred architecture of the nineteenth and twentieth centuries reflects the ongoing struggle between religion and rationalism.

The Romantics provided a German alternative to the rationalism of antiquity with their focus on the art and architecture of the Middle Ages, and specifically of the late Gothic period. Even as early as 1773 Goethe wrote of his admiration for Strasburg Cathedral, and in 1814, Joseph Görres spearheaded the campaign for the completion of Cologne Cathedral, where construction had not taken place since 1560. In addition to classicism and Gothic influences, other historical periods also came into play. References to Romanesque, Early Christian, and Byzantine models in sacred buildings sprang in part from a renewed interest in the origins of Christianity, but also from a growing appreciation for regional heritage. The new cathedral built in Berlin, which was designed to rival St Paul's in London, is a Protestant adaptation of the neo-baroque style of St Peter's in Rome.

Toward the end of the nineteenth century, the impossibility of unifying all of the disparate formal languages of the various historical eras led many young artists to reject outright what they called "style architecture." Vienna was one of the early centers of the anti-academic movement, and it was there that the secessionists united against historicism's artificial pathos and stodgy formalism.

One of the protagonists of this movement was the Viennese architect Otto Wagner. He began as a historicist, but his focus shifted toward clear, functional, technically advanced architectural design. In Barcelona, Antoni Gaudí started with a Gothic ground plan to design the utterly idiosyncratic and innovative La Sagrada Familia (Holy Family), which is still a work in progress today. Later in the century there was a revival of rationalism, in which sober, functional structures such as factories, power planets, and warehouses came to the fore, and religious architecture was less interesting. The mystical visions of the expressionist school, a reaction to the horror of World War I, brought churches and other sacred buildings back into the spotlight. These visionary works of religous architecture were often influenced by Gothic models, but executed in new materials such as reinforced concrete. In 1901, Jules Astruc completed the revolutionary Notre-Dame-du-Travail in Paris's fourteenth arrondissement. In Germany, the work of Dominikus Böhm and Rudolf Schwarz attained a similar, near perfect synthesis of rational and sensual forms. Le Corbusier's pilgrimage church at Ronchamp, France, remains one of a kind even today. This walk-in sculpture is an expressive, dynamic masterpiece of the art of building with concrete.

In the 1970s and 1980s, multifunctional sacred spaces free of churchly decor specific to a particular sect or denomination became increasingly popular. It was only toward the very end of the twentieth century that the tide turned again, and a movement toward the "reconsecration" of sacred architecture gained force. Allmann Sattler Wappner's 1998 Herz Jesu Kirche (Sacred Heart Church) in Munich showed that even an avant-garde building can also be imbued with spiritual values.

Above: **Munich,** Herz Jesu (Sacred Heart), architecture group Allmann Sattler Wappner, 1998, interior.

Left: **Hasloch am Main, Germany,** St Josef, *The Risen Christ,* wood sculpture by Julius Brausenwein, 1958.

Opposite: **Le Raincy, near Paris,** Notre-Dame-du-Travail, Jules Astruc, 1899–1901, interior.

Above: **Paris,** Ste-Clotilde, Franz Gau
and Théodore Ballu, designed 1833,
constructed 1845–1866, interior.

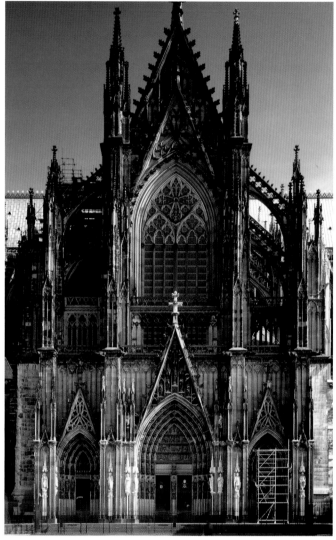

Above: **Cologne,** cathedral, completed
by Ernst Friedrich Zwirner and Richard
Voigtel 1842–1880, facade of the
south transept.

Paris, Ste-Clotilde

Ste-Clotilde was Paris's first completely new "Gothic" church of
the nineteenth century. Design and construction were supervised
from beginning to end by the École des Beaux-Arts, which called
for the use of historicist formal elements well within the bounds
of "good taste" in all arts and crafts. The first design, by Théodore
Ballu, was heavily criticized. German architect Franz Christian
Gau was brought in from Cologne to start from scratch. The
twin-towered, three-story facade of the finished church is a direct
reference to thirteenth-century French architecture, yet without
remaining true to the actual tradition. Architectural historians and
critics from the Beaux-Arts school were largely unhappy with the
result. Later, the innovations of Eugène Viollet-le-Duc would lead
to a freer, more constructive interpretation of the Gothic style.

Cologne Cathedral

In Germany, the recovery of the original plans for the tower
facade of Cologne's largely unfinished cathedral gave fresh wind
to the German Romantics in their quest for nationalist and
religious sentiment. In 1814, journalist and scholar Joseph
Görres called for the cathedral to finally be completed—it had
been standing with incomplete towers since 1560. Now, it
would become a "symbol of the new empire." Work only began
again in earnest in 1842 under the direction of chief architect
Ernst Friedrich Zwirner. In 1861 the transept was finished, and
by 1863 the interior had been renovated. In 1880, the completion of the towers was celebrated with great ceremony.
Throughout construction, the precepts of the original medieval
plan were followed as closely as possible.

Above: **Remagen, Germany**,
St Apollinaris, Ernst Friedrich Zwirner,
1839–1843, exterior view.

Above: **Munich,** Mariahilfkirche,
Joseph Daniel Ohlmüller,1831–1839,
exterior after 1953 reconstruction;
decoration was kept to a minimum.

Remagen, St Apollinaris

Three years before taking charge of the reconstruction of the Cologne Cathedral, Ernst Friedrich Zwirner laid the corner-stone of another masterpiece of German neogothic architecture.

At Remagen, Zwirner was able to work with Gothic forms without the need to comply with a pre-existing medieval building or plan. He decided on a Greek cross plan, with two slender towers flanking the small polygonal eastern choir in addition to the traditional pair of towers on the west facade. His choice of a nearly central-plan building, together with his free interpretation of Gothic decorative motifs, is similar to Karl Friedrich Schinkel's approach to historicist styles. Zwirner's work, however, reveals a much more idealized conception of the Middle Ages.

Munich, Mariahilfkirche (Mariahilf Church)

Over the course of the nineteenth century, knowledge of design, engineering, and construction multiplied exponentially. But while King Ludwig I of Bavaria reigned, there was little interest in what was new. What the king wanted were buildings that followed historical models as closely as possible.

Mariahilf Church, by architect Joseph Daniel Ohlmüller, is one of these. The choir and west tower of the three-aisled hall church are polygonal in plan, exactly as they would have been in the late Gothic period. The broken-base pediment is a reference to Freiburg Cathedral. In 1944, the predominantly brick Mariahilf was heavily damaged by Allied air raids. It was rebuilt in a simplified form in 1953. Its original, uniquely beautiful stained glass windows could not be restored.

Berlin Cathedral

Planning for Berlin Cathedral began during the reign of Emperor Frederich III, who appointed Julius Karl Raschdorff as its architect, but the project was seen to completion by Wilhelm II. Completed in 1905, the cathedral was designed to serve as a center of Prussian, if not German, Protestantism.

The ambitious neobaroque plan was designed to rival St Peter's in Rome, St Paul's in London, and especially the newly completed Cologne Cathedral, a bastion of German Catholicism. This ideological overload is visible in the somewhat overdramatic stylistic tendencies of the massively domed building. Berlin Cathedral continues to serve as both a congregational and community church. It is also the final resting place of the Hohenzollern emperors.

Opposite: **Berlin,** cathedral, Julius Karl Raschdorff, 1894–1905, partially reconstructed after World War II.

Munich, Ludwigskirche (St Louis)

In addition to classical and Gothic models, other historicist styles were also in evidence. Leo von Klenze and Friedrich von Gärtner designed an ensemble of historicist buildings for King Ludwig of Bavaria, most of them influenced by Italian buildings dating from the Romanesque period to the early Renaissance. These include Ludwigskirche, as well as the state library, university, Feldherrenhalle (Field Marshall's Hall), and the Siegestor (Victory Gate).

The church has a twin-towered facade with flanking arcades. The choir is decorated with a fresco of the Last Judgment by Peter Cornelius, which is the largest wall painting of the nineteenth century.

Above and right: **Munich,** Ludwigskirche, Friedrich von Gärtner, 1829–1844, interior and facade facing Leopoldstraße.

broad west facade with its powerful towers. This monumental building, where even the joins between the blocks were individually designed, was finally completed in 1990 with the laying of the last finial.

Although the neogothic style dominated sacred architecture, there were other historicist options available. Henry Hobson Richardson, for example, designed Boston's Trinity Church with rounded entry portals and solid towers reminiscent of the Romanesque period in southern France. Some even tried to mix styles. The Cathedral of St John the Divine in New York City, designed by Heins & Lafarge in 1892, began as a Byzantine-Romanesque-early Gothic conglomeration with a high Gothic facade. After the 1907 death of George Lewis Heins, the new architect, Ralph Adams Cram, tried to bring a greater stylistic unity to the unfinished building, and his neogothic plan was closer to the medieval model. Ideally, the radical change in plan should have meant that certain parts of what had already been built would be torn down. This has yet to take place, and the cathedral, including its towering facade, remains incomplete today.

Historicist Churches in the USA

Historicism met with great success in the United States. Sacred architecture in North America, as in Europe, has been dominated by neogothic and other medieval styles, as evidenced by thousands of churches all over the country. Its aura unbroken, neogothic is still the preferred style for cathedrals and parish churches today.

Richard Upjohn was a British furniture maker who settled in Boston after immigrating in 1829. Although he began as a strict neoclassicist, he became the pioneer of American Gothic Revival architecture. Upjohn designed Trinity Church in New York City (1841–1846), as well as many other churches. James Renwick's St Patrick's Cathedral, once the tallest building in New York, was no less significant. From the laying of the cornerstone, both the architect and his patrons were determined to create a "Gothic cathedral" on the level of the best Europe could offer. Today, this proud structure is almost completely overwhelmed by surrounding skyscrapers.

The National Cathedral in Washington D.C. was redesigned many times. Its original plan dates from 1891 and was the work of George Frederick Bodley. After his death, Henry Vaughn stepped in, followed by Philip Frohman. Frohman designed the

Vienna, Kirche am Steinhof (St Leopold)

The generation of artists coming of age at the end of the nineteenth century looked for a way past the clutter of historicist styles. In Vienna, Otto Wagner promoted a new, functional, and technically innovative architecture. One of his most influential works is the 1902 design for the Kirche am Steinhof (St Leopold). The supremely functional building located on the grounds of a psychiatric asylum includes special accommodations for both the spiritual and physical needs of the patients.

The church is essentially a Byzantine-style dome on cross, which visually crowns the entire, terraced complex. The construction is steel frame, with marble facades. The generous interior space is pristine white, with delicate gold delineating the coffers of the vault. Wagner worked in close collaboration with stained glass artist Koloman Moser and mosaicist Remigius Geyler. Sculptors Carl Ederer and Othmar Schimkowitz created the high altar and other sculpture. High-quality materials together with Wagner's subtle, iconographic visual language are balm to the senses.

The exterior of the church, with its dome visible from far away, is a symbol of the early twentieth century resurgence of Roman Catholicism in Vienna.

Below: **Vienna,** Kirche am Steinhof (St Leopold), Otto Wagner, 1902–1907, interior.

Barcelona, La Sagrada Familia (Holy Family)

The dream of an eccentric, or the last Gothic cathedral? La Sagrada Familia is a curiosity. Its architect, Antoni Gaudí took his ideas for the cathedral's completion to the grave. At the time of his death in 1926, only the east facade was standing. The west and south facades existed only in plan. Work on La Sagrada Familia halted until the 1950s, when Gaudí's masterpiece was taken up again, funded almost entirely by public donations.

Gaudí's "church to atone for the excesses of the time" was designed to compete with Cologne Cathedral and Reims Cathedral. There are some similarities in plan. All three are five-aisled long-nave churches with three-aisled transepts. La Sagrada Familia is nearly as tall as Cologne Cathedral, though its eighteen (!) satellite towers go far beyond anything built so far. The elevations of La Sagrada Familia break with all existing conventions. Gaudí invented a new, revolutionary support system based on forms found in nature that made it unnecessary to build flying buttresses. Thus, slanted beams transfer the thrust of the vaults directly to the foundations.

La Sagrada Familia is a dogma of the Christian faith in stone. Three monumental facades are

dedicated to the life of Christ: his birth, his passion, and his glory in the kingdom of heaven. The narrow parabolic towers are also conceptually integrated. The tallest tower in the center symbolizes Christ the savior. The apse tower is his mother, Mary, with the four towers between them representing the four evangelists. The facade towers, twelve in all, symbolize the twelve apostles.

Left and above: **Barcelona,** La Sagrada Familia, beg. 1882 from a design by Antoni Gaudí, still under construction.

Above: **Copenhagen,**
Grundtvig's Church, Peder
Vilhelm Jensen-Klint and Kaare
Klint, 1913, 1921–1940,
exterior.

Copenhagen, Grundtvig's Church

The expressionistic brick of Grundtvig's Church is a brilliant paraphrase of traditional Gothic architecture. The church is the work of architect-engineer Peder Vilhelm Jensen-Klint, who admired the "subtle, honest forms" of Danish village churches. In Grundtvig's Church, he tried to translate that simplicity into a contemporary formal language. His building is a basilical plan, similar to the local medieval parish churches, but is fronted not by a simple portal, but a monumental west facade.

The verticality of Gothic architecture becomes a distinctive aesthetic impulse. It dominates the oversize elements of the facade and gables and continues in the decoration, where brickwork pilaster strips are arrayed "like organ pipes". Jensen-Klint completed his plan in 1913, winning a competition to design the church. Construction could not begin until 1921, after the end of the First World War. Following the 1936 death of the architect, his son, Kaare Klint, oversaw the project. Although the church was in use from 1927, it was not completed until 1940.

Grundvig's Church is named for Nikolai Severin Grundtvig, a famous Danish poet, scholar and reform theologian.

Berlin, Kirche am Hohenzollernplatz (Church on Hohenzollernplatz)

The mystical worldview of the expressionists was born of the horrors of the First World War. Expressionism infused sacred architecture with new impulses and inspiration. However, although architects and graphic artists put down their visions on paper, their realization was rare. Otto Bartning's famous Sternkirche (Star Church) was conceived as a symbolic representation of the cosmos. But the expressionists did not see their work as mere utopian fantasy. In their designs for churches, they were united in the effort to produce a totally new, contemporary version of community space. Churches were not just empty space, but "healing, sacred places" where religious ideas were communally celebrated.

One of the few expressionist church designs actually built was Fritz Höger's Kirche on Hohenzollernplatz in Berlin. As in all his works, the church, constructed between 1930 and 1933, is both visually striking and supremely functional. The brick building has a steel frame structure. The massive stair towers flank a bold facade enhanced by gilding between the bricks. Stained glass adds emotional heft to both the exterior and the interior, where thirteen ogival reinforced concrete beams bridge the nave like Gothic arches. Colored light from the windows streams in between them, giving the interior an almost supernatural quality.

Opposite: **Berlin,** Kirche am
Hohenzollernplatz, Fritz Höger,
1930–1933, interior.

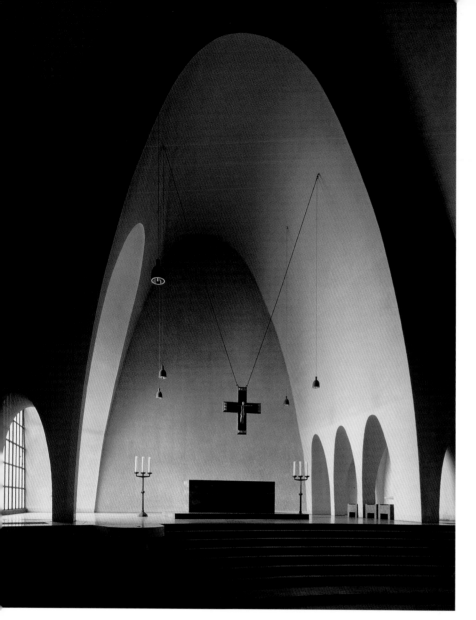

Cologne, St Engelbert

Architect Dominikus Böhm understood light as a building material given to us by God, and employed it as such. His St Engelbert in Cologne was constructed between 1930 and 1932. Böhm's dramatic direction of natural light leads the eye to a sanctuary whose center is drenched in daylight that breaks in from the side and throws strong shadows. In contrast, the circular space for the congregation is dimly lit. High above, hidden lighting dramatically illuminates the concrete vault, and catches the radiating ribs to suggest a heavenly glow.

Dominikus Böhm revived Catholic sacred buildings in more ways than one. True to the maxim of one God, one community, one place, his groundbreaking churches were usually centrally-planned buildings, and the area around the altar was often given a mystical effect through dramatic architectural direction and use of light. At the same time, Böhm was a virtuoso at making the most of the structural and aesthetic possibilities of new technologies and materials, such as reinforced concrete. In St Engelbert, he uses variations on the parabolic form both as his support elements, and at the same time as a physical embodiment of the "raising up" of Christ after the resurrection. The parabolic forms are repeated in the church's exterior, a visual and symbolic reference to their dominance within.

Above and right: **Cologne,** St Engelbert, Dominikus Böhm, 1930–1932, interior and exterior views.

Aachen, Fronleichnam (Corpus Christi)

Rudolf Schwarz, a student of Hans Poelzig, was the second great German church architect of the 1930s and early postwar period. Like Dominikus Böhm, a friend and occasional colleague, Schwarz recrafted sacred space as a multifunctional realm where a community could gather and share their experience of faith. In contrast to Böhm's expressionist tendencies and emotionalism, Schwarz's style was overwhelmingly rationalistic and severe. Mystical light effects and dramatically directed architecture had no place in his work.

Schwartz's Fronleichnam Church in Aachen is the starting point for all his later work. Through an extended, conflict-ridden design process, he devised a model that was sober and unpretentious, but also aesthetically impressive. His design solution was a kind of God factory. Corpus Christi's dominating element is a simple, modest rectilinear room. The plain glass nave windows—his churches have between five and twelve on each long wall—are the only decorative element, bringing diffuse light into the bare interior through unadorned openings. Daylight from the windows in one side falls on the opposite wall, visually reducing the monotony of plain white space. The walls become almost transparent, a membrane between inside and outside, or between this life and the next.

After the end of World War II, more churches were built in Europe than ever before and Rudolf Schwartz was highly sought after. He remained true to his original conception, although his early buildings, like Corpus Christi in Aachen, are among his best.

Above and left: **Aachen,** Fronleichnam, Rudolf Schwartz, 1929–1930, interior and exterior views.

Ronchamp, Notre-Dame-du-Haut
(Our Lady on High)

Notre-Dame-du-Haut in Ronchamp, France, is a milestone of modern sacred architecture and a masterpiece of twentieth-century architecture. Nonconformist architect Charles-Édouard Jeanneret, who called himself Le Corbusier, created a powerful pilgrimage church that is both a site for meditation and a walk-through sculpture in itself. Organically integrated into the hilly landscape of southwest France, Notre-Dame-du-Haut's curving concrete roof is its dominant visual element, dramatically set off by its white fieldstone walls. The interior is also white. Colored shafts of light entering through slit windows enhance the contemplative atmosphere of the space.

Above and right: **Ronchamp,** pilgrimage church Notre-Dame-du-Haut, Le Corbusier, 1953–1955, interior and exterior.

Brasília

In the 1940s, while nearly all of Europe, North America, and Asia were embroiled in World War II, Modernism was able to develop freely in South and Central America. In Brazil, progressive president Juscelino Kubitschek made modern architecture the national style when he commissioned the new capital city of Brasília. Lucio Costa, tasked with designing an urban utopia in the middle of the Amazon in the undeveloped high plains of Goías, devised the famous *Pilot Plan Brasília* that formed the basis for the organization of the new city. It was Oscar Niemeyer who gave it its avant-garde look. Between 1958 and 1970, in addition to several grandiose government buildings, Niemeyer designed one of the most unusual sacred buildings of all time, a cathedral that vaguely resembles a crown of thorns. The National Cathedral was built in record time—just two years—with the help of sixteen hyperbolic precast concrete columns. Set in a circle, the massive columns are sunk into the earth for nearly half their length. Brightly colored abstract stained glass windows by artist Antônia Marianne Peretti fill the space between them, filling the otherwise almost empty interior with soft blue light. Interior decorative elements are few, and include Alfredo Ceschiatti's three monumental angel sculptures

that hover in the air high above the altar, suspended from the dome. The four larger-than-life-size images of the evangelists in front of the cathedral are by the same artist.

Also in Brasília is the Santuário Dom Bosco, also known as the Blue Church. Long acknowledged as one of the most atmospheric of all modern sacred buildings, the Blue Church is located in a residential area in the south of the capital. Eighty concrete beams, each 52 feet (16 m) long, form pointed arches over a monumental interior space. Stained glass windows in twelve different shades of blue filter the streaming sunlight, bathing the interior in an unearthly light. A chandelier suspended on almost 12 feet (3.5 m) of steel cable hangs from the center of the ceiling, radiating the light of 180 bulbs and over 7,000 crystals.

The Blue Church was erected in honor of Dom Giovanni Bosco (1815–1888), Italian founder of the Salesian order. Don Bosco had a vision of a new civilization rising in a land flowing with milk and honey, located between 15 and 20 degrees latitude. Seventy-five years later Lúcio Costa und Oscar Niemeyer built the utopian city of Brasília in exactly this region. Don Bosco, who was made a saint in 1934, was declared its patron.

Opposite top and bottom: **Brasília**, National Cathedral, Oscar Niemeyer, 1958–1970, view into the "dome" and exterior.

Above: **Brasília,** Santuário Dom Bosco (Blue Church), Carlos Antonio Narves, consecrated in 1970.

Modern Churches in the USA

After the neoromanesque Cathedral of San Francisco was destroyed by fire in 1962, planning began for a new building in a decidedly modern form—an exception in North America, where even in the twentieth century, strong historicist leanings remained the rule in sacred architecture. It is thanks to the daring of Archbishop Joseph McGucken that the architect Pier Luigi Nervi, a representation of rationalist architecture, was allowed to execute the project. The reforms of the Second Vatican Council had paved the way and led to that possibility. Nervi and his colleague in Boston, Pietro Belluschi, created a path-breaking concrete structure that rests on four pedestals. Above them, a cruciform supporting structure rises almost 90 feet (27 m), and the four massive, freestanding parabloids that form the roof are held by it. Above the altar is a kinetic aluminum sculpture by Richard Lippold that symbolizes the connection between God and humanity.

A further milestone in modern church architecture in the USA is Philip Johnson's Crystal Cathedral in Garden Grove, California. It, too, for all its modernity, is infused with symbolic qualities. A steel construction encased by about 10,000 glass windows towers above a star-shaped floor plan. Silicon joinings ensure that the glass building is able to withstand even powerful earthquakes.

A recent sacred construction project on a grand scale is the work of Spanish architect Rafael Moneo. He designed the new Los Angeles Cathedral, which replaces a forerunner destroyed by an earthquake in 1994, though not in the same location. Moneo's block-like concrete structure plays with echoes of Early Christian or Romanesque basilicas, but their axial orientation and structuring principles are absent.

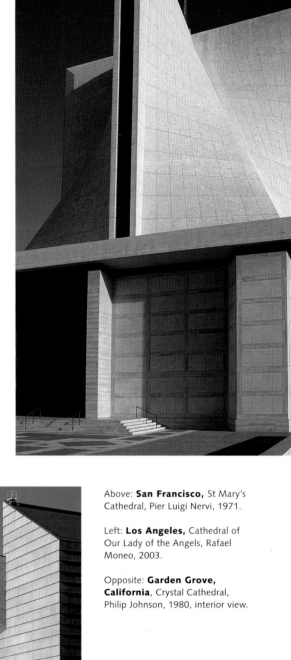

Above: **San Francisco,** St Mary's Cathedral, Pier Luigi Nervi, 1971.

Left: **Los Angeles,** Cathedral of Our Lady of the Angels, Rafael Moneo, 2003.

Opposite: **Garden Grove, California**, Crystal Cathedral, Philip Johnson, 1980, interior view.

Index of Illustrations

Aachen, minster 22
— Fronleichnam (Corpus Christi) 249
Albi, Cathedral of Ste-Cécile 105
Amiens, Cathedral of Notre-Dame 98–99
Anet Lodge 189
Angoulême, Cathedral of St-Pierre 61
Antwerp, Cathedral of Our Lady 132
Assisi, S. Francesco (St Francis) 148
Aulnay-de-Saintonge, former collegiate
    church St-Pierre-de-la-Tour 64
Autun, St-Lazare 56-57
Auxerre, Cathedral of St-Étienne 101

Banz, Benedictine abbey church 228
Barcelona, cathedral 163
— Sagrada Família 245
— Sta. Maria del Mar 162
Bari, S. Nicola 46
Basel, minster 128
Batalha, Monastery of S. Maria
    da Vitoria 166
Belém (Lisbon), Jerónimos Monastery 167
Bergamo, Cappella Colleoni at
    S. Maria Maggiore 184
Berlin, cathedral 241
— Church on Hohenzollernplatz 247
Bern, minster 129
Birnau, Church of Our Lady 231
Bologna, S. Francesco 149
— S. Petronio 157
Borgund, stave church 78–79
Boston, Trinity Church 242
Bourg-en-Bresse, Brou Abbey Church 107
Bourges, Cathedral of St-Étienne 94–95
Bra, S. Chiara 201
Braga, Bom Jesus do Monte 212
Brasília, cathedral 252
— Santuário Dom Bosco (Blue Church) 253
Breslau, Elector's Chapel 220–221
Brussels, St Johann Baptist 218
Burgos, cathedral 158–159

Caen, Ste-Trinité 53
— St-Étienne 52
Cambridge, King's College Chapel 147
Canterbury, cathedral 138
Carcassonne, Cathedral of St-Nazaire 80
Cardona, St Vicenç 66–67
Cefalù, cathedral 49
— view of city 48–49
Cerisy-la-Forêt, St-Vigor 53
Charlieu, ehem. Prioratskirche
    St-Fortunat 64
Chartres, cathedral 90–93
Chorin, former Cistercian abbey
    church 119
Coimbra, Sé Velha (Old Cathedral) 73
Cologne, cathedral 4, 114–115, 238
— St Aposteln 35
— St Engelbert 248
— St Maria im Kapitol 35, 65
— St Pantaleon 29
Como, S. Abbondio 39
Conques, Ste-Foy 55
Constance, Minster of Our Lady 25
Copenhagen, Grundtvig's Church 246
Córdoba, Argentina, cathedral 216
Corvey, former abbey church 23
Coutances, cathedral 100

Delft, Nieuwe Kerk (New Church) 133
Dijon, Abbey Church of St-Bénigne 65
Dresden, Frauenkirche (Church of Our
    Lady) 234–235
Durham, cathedral 74

Einsiedeln, Benedictine abbey church 229
Ely, cathedral 74–75

Florence, Baptistery of St John 45
— campanile 152
— cathedral 152, 172
— S. Croce 150-151

— S. Lorenzo 173
— S. Maria Novella 151, 175
— S. Miniato al Monte 44
— S. Spirito 172
Fontenay, abbey church 62
Fontevraud, former abbey church 61
Fountains Abbey, former Cistercian
    abbey 77
Freiberg, Goldene Pforte
    (Golden Gate) 65
Freiburg, cathedral 112–113
Frómista, S. Martín 69
Fulda, St Michael 24

Garden Grove, CA, Crystal Cathedral 255
Gdansk (Danzig), St Mary 137
Gernrode, St Cyriacus 26–27
Gloucester, cathedral 144–145
Granada, Carthusian abbey church 211
Guadalajara, Mexico, cathedral 215

Hamburg, St Michael 234
Hasloch am Main, St Josef 237
Havana, Cuba, cathedral 214
Hildesheim, St Michael 20, 26

Istanbul, Hagia Sophia 16–17

Jerez de la Frontera, Carthusian
    Abbey Church Nuestra Señora
    de la Defensión 208
Jerusalem, Church of the Holy Sepulcher 10

Kappel, pilgrimage chapel 228
Kleinkomburg, St Ägidius (St Giles) 19

La Seu d'Urgell, cathedral 66
Landshut, St Martin 125
Laon, Cathedral of Notre-Dame 88–89
Legum Abbey 135
León, cathedral 160–161
Le Raincy, Notre-Dame-du-Travail 238
Limburg an der Lahn, cathedral 36–37
Lincoln, cathedral 138, 143
London, St Paul's Cathedral 219
— Westminster Abbey 142
Lorsch, gatehouse 22
Los Angeles, Cathedral of Our Lady
    of the Angels 254
Löwen, Belgium, St Michael 218
Løgumkloster 135
Lübeck, Marienkirche (Church of St Mary)
    81, 118
Lund, Norway, cathedral 78

Mainz, Cathedral of St Martin and
    St Stephan 32
Mantua, S. Andrea 174–175
Marburg an der Lahn, St Elisabeth 109
Maria Laach 34
Melk, Austria, Benedictine Abbey 226–227
Mexico City, cathedral 214
Milan, cathedral 156–157
— S. Ambrogio 38-39
— S. Lorenzo 13
— S. Maria delle Grazie 179
Modena, Cathedral of S. Geminiano 42
Moissac, Abbey Church of St-Pierre 65
Monreale, cathedral 48
Montepulciano, S. Biagio 176
Munich, Frauenkirche 124–125
— Herz Jesu 237
— Ludwigskirche 240
— Mariahilfkirche 239
— St Michael 222
Murcia, cathedral 208
Müstair, St John 22

Naples, Foro Murat 203
Narbonne, Cathedral of St-Just 105
Naumburg, Cathedral of St Peter
    and St Paul 116–117
Neresheim, abbey church 191, 233
New York, St Patrick's Cathedral 243
Norwich, Cathedral of the Holy Trinity 76

Odense, Cathedral of St Canute 134

Orvieto, cathedral 154–155
Ouro Preto, Brazil, São Francisco
    de Assis 217

Palermo, cathedral 48
Palma de Mallorca, cathedral 162
Paray-le-Monial, priory church 59
Paris, Cathedral of Notre-Dame 86–87
— Church of the Sorbonne 204
— La Madeleine 206–207
— Les Invalides 204
— Panthéon 207
— St-Étienne-du-Mont 188
— St-Eustache 188–189
— Ste-Chapelle 102–103
— Ste-Clotilde 238
Parma, baptistery 43
— cathedral 43
Périgueux, Cathedral of St-Front 61
Peterborough, cathedral 141
Pisa, Campo del Miracoli, cathedral 45
— S. Maria della Spina 155
Pontigny, abbey church 63
Porto, Igreja dos Grilos 213
— Torre dos Clérigos 213
Possagno, Tempio Canoviano 202–203
Prague, Cathedral of St Vitus 130–131
Prato, S. Maria delle Carceri 176
Prenzlau, Marienkirche (Church of
    St Mary) 118

Quedlinburg, St Servatius 65

Ratzeburg, Cathedral of St Maria and
    St John the Evangelist 36
Ravenna, S. Vitale 9, 14–15
Regensburg, cathedral 120
Reims, Cathedral of Notre Dame 96–97
— St-Rémi 50
Remagen, St Apollinaris 239
Rievaulx Abbey, former Cistercian
    abbey 77
Rimini, Tempio Malatestiano 168
Rio de Janeiro, Monastery of
    São Bento 217
Rome, Il Gesù 194
— Old St Peter's 10
— S. Agnese 197
— S. Andrea al Quirinale 195
— S. Andrea delle Fratte 196
— S. Constanza 9, 11
— S. Ivo alla Sapienza 190
— S. Maria in Campitelli 198
— S. Pietro in Montorio 178–179
— S. Sabina 11
— S. Susanna 194
— SS. Luca e Martina 199
— St Peter's 169, 180–183
Ronchamp, Notre-Dame-du-Haut
    (Our Lady on High) 250–251
Rouen, St-Ouen 106

Salamanca, New Cathedral 165
— S. Esteban 191, 210
Salem, former Cistercian abbey church
    81, 121
Salisbury, cathedral 140
Salzburg, cathedral 223
— Dreifaltigkeitskirche (Holy Trinity
    Church) 225
— Collegiate Church 225
San Francisco, St Mary's Cathedral 254
Santa Fe, Argentina, S. Francisco 216
Santiago de Compostela,
    cathedral 68, 209
Schwäbisch-Gmünd, Church of the
    Holy Cross 123
Segovia, Iglesia de la Vera Cruz 72
Semur-en-Brionnais, St-Hilaire 64
Sens, St-Étienne Cathedral 106
Serrabone, Notre-Dame 65
Seville, cathedral 164–165
Siena, cathedral 153
Solothurn, Jesuit church 229

Speyer, Cathedral of St Mary and
    St Stephen 30–31
St-Denis, cathedral 84–85
St-Genis-des-Fontaines 64
St-Germain-en-Laye, Ste-Chapelle 102
St-Savin-sur-Gartempe 60
Stargard Szczecinski, Church of
    the Blessed Virgin 136–137
Steinbach, sog. Einhardsbasilika 25
Steinhausen, St Peter and Paul 230
S. Domingo de Silos 65
Stockholm, Riddarholmen Church 220
Strasbourg, minster 2, 110–111

Thessaloniki, Hagios Demetrios 12
Todi, S. Fortunato 149
— S. Maria della Consolazione 177
Toledo, cathedral 160, 210
Tomar, Templar Church 72
Toro, Collegiate Church of S. María
    la Mayor 70
Toulouse, Church of the Jacobins 104
— St-Sernin 54, 64
Tournus, St-Philibert 50–51
Trani, S. Nicola Pellegrino 47
Trier, Cathedral of St Peter 28
— former Collegiate Church of Our
    Dear Lady 108
— Palatine Chapel 8
Turin, La Superga 200
— S. Lorenzo 200

Ulm, minster 122
Uppsala, cathedral 135
Utrecht, Cathedral of St Martin 133

Venice, Il Redentore 187
— S. Giorgio Maggiore 186–187
— S. Marco 40–41
— S. Maria dei Miracoli 185
Verona, S. Zeno Maggiore 40
Versailles, Royal Chapel 205
Vézelay, Ste-Madeleine 18, 58
Vienna, Karlskirche (St Charles Borromeo)
    224–225
— Kirche am Steinhof (St Leopold) 244
— Stephansdom 126–127
Vierzehnheiligen, Germany, pilgrimage
    church 232–33

Washington D.C., National Cathedral 242
Weingarten, abbey church 229
Wells, cathedral 139, 141
Winchester, cathedral 146
Worms, Cathedral of St Peter 33
Wroclaw, see Breslau

Zamora, cathedral 71

Picture credits

p. 10: Scala, Florence
p. 72 top right: Joseph Martin, Madrid
pp. 130/131: Markus Hilbich, Berlin
pp. 136/137: Florian Monheim, Bildarchiv
    Monheim, Krefeld
p. 148: Scala, Florence
p. 219: A. F. Kersting, London
pp. 216/217, 252/253: Pablo de la Riestra
p. 244: Zugmann Fotografie KEG, Vienna

Additional permission to reproduce:
For pp. 116/117: © Vereinigte Domstifter
    zu Merseburg und Naumburg
    (reproduction forbidden)
For pp. 250/251: © FLC/VB Bild-Kunst,
    Bonn 2007
For pp. 214/215, 242/243, 254/255:
    © Corbis

All other images: Achim Bednorz, Cologne